Child Labor Today

A Human Rights Issue

Child Labor Today

A Human Rights Issue

ISSUES IN FOCUS TODAY

Wendy Herumin

Enslow Publishers, Inc.
40 Industrial Road
Box 398
Berkeley Heights, NJ 07922
USA

http://www.enslow.com

Dedicated to Gwendolyn Lea Herzstein,
a staunch supporter of children's rights.

Library of Congress Cataloging-in-Publication Data

Herumin, Wendy.
     Child labor today : a human rights issue / Wendy Herumin.
        p. cm. — (Issues in focus today)
     Includes bibliographical references and index.
     ISBN-13: 978-0-7660-2682-7
     ISBN-10: 0-7660-2682-5
     1. Child labor—Juvenile literature. 2. Human rights—Juvenile literature. I. Title.
     HD6231.H47 2007
     331.3'1—dc22
                                                            2007010625

Printed in the United States of America

10 9 8 7 6 5 4 3 2 1

Photo Credits: AP/Wide World, pp. 11, 34, 57, 60, 63, 72, 79, 85, 89, 95, 101, 103; Paula
Bronstein/Getty Images, p. 40; Getty Images, pp. 5, 28, 66, 83, 105; Tim Graham/Getty
Images, p. 7; The Image Works, pp. 3, 5, 24, 45, 48, 52, 54, 74, 99; Library of Congress,
pp. 17, 22, 93; National Archives and Records Administration, pp. 5, 19; Per-Anders
Pettersson/Getty Images, pp. 5, 70; Tom Stoddart Archive/Getty Images, pp. 5, 14, 42, 97.

Cover Photo: The Image Works.

Contents

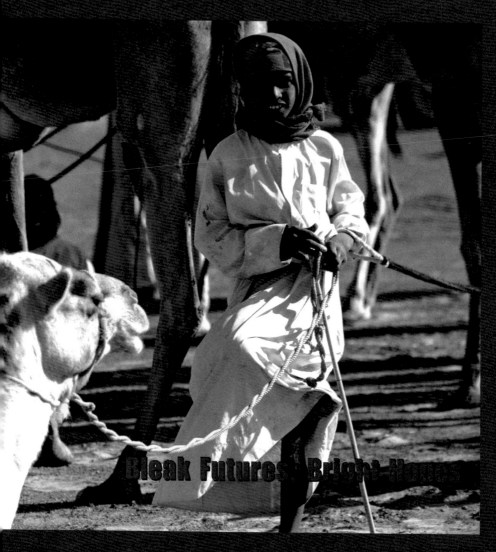

Bleak Futures, Bright Hopes

Camel racing season in the United Arab Emirates stretches from November to April. The sport began centuries ago when Bedouin tribes raced their camels across scorching sands. Today camels run on outdoor tracks at speeds of up to twenty-five miles per hour. Many Arab countries encourage camel racing to honor their cultural heritage.

A harsher side to the sport captured world attention in recent years. Public outrage grew in the late 1990s over the practice of using children as camel jockeys. Human rights groups reported that some riders were as young as four years old.[1] Although most Arab countries had banned the use of underage jockeys, children still rode in races. Officials did not stop them. Child jockeys raced in Kuwait, Qatar, Oman, and Sudan.[2]

Human rights groups reported that young boys were strapped on top of camels. Most camels were three times as tall as their riders and weighed up to six hundred pounds. A fall could mean broken arms or legs for a child—or worse. In 2004, a five-year-old boy was crushed beneath the hooves of a galloping herd during training.[3] He later died at the hospital.

Ansar Burney, a lawyer from Pakistan, led a campaign to stop the use of child jockeys. Investigators found many abuses. Boys lived in camps surrounded by barbed wire.[4] Toddlers as young as two years old lived in the camps.[5] The boys were starved to keep their weight low.[6]

Burney's organization reported one of the "advantages" of using children. When boys screamed in pain or terror, the camels ran faster.[7] Burney was outraged over the cruelty of the camel trainers.

"Children as young as two and a half years are used and abused by these people without regret of their actions or any fear of god," Burney said.[8]

In 2004, the United Arab Emirates opened a center for young camel jockeys. The government made new, tougher laws. International organizations could finally rescue boys from the racing camps and return them to their homes in Bangladesh, Pakistan, and Sudan. Neighboring countries Oman and Qatar also joined the fight.

Today a technological innovation is helping to keep children off the backs of racing camels. Robots introduced into the United Arab Emirates in 2005 are proving to be successful substitutes for human jockeys. A newspaper article in 2007 described the new face of camel racing.[9] Now animals and humans can race side by side. Camels and their robotic riders gallop on a traditional racetrack while human owners drive on a paved road alongside their four-legged "stars." The humans use remote control devices to give commands to the robots. Dressed like human jockeys, the robots can crack a whip as fiercely as a boy. Early robots weighed between thirty-three and sixty pounds—the typical weight range of a healthy seven-year-old child—but newer versions weigh closer to six pounds, according to the report.[10]

Children at Risk

Many child jockeys involved in camel racing were victims of a practice known as *trafficking*, according to the U.S. State Department. A trafficked person is moved from one place to another and forced to work—often in slave-like conditions. Trafficking may involve transporting a child from one country to another or relocating the child within the same country, such as from a sparsely populated village to a larger city. Trafficking patterns reflect supply and demand, according to Catherine Chen, trafficking specialist for Save the Children, an international relief and development agency. She explains that trafficking is primarily an economic activity. Trafficking agents simply go "where there's money," says Chen.[11] For example, a girl from a small African farming village might be taken to the home of a wealthier family in a seaport city to cook, clean, and care for small children. The trafficking agent earns a sum of money for delivering the child to her employers, but the girl will likely receive no more than room and board in exchange for her labor.

The U.S. State Department says the most important aspect of trafficking is not the movement of a person from one place to another but the *force or deception* used to make someone work:

The child sold by his parents to the owner of a brick kiln on the outskirts of his rural Indian village is a trafficking victim. And, so is the Mexican man who legally or illegally migrates to the United

States, only to be threatened and beaten by his agricultural crew leader to keep him from leaving the job.[12]

Work that involves trafficking is one of the worst forms of child labor, according to the International Labour Organization, or ILO. (This United Nations agency uses the British spelling of the word "labor.") The ILO maintains an organization—IPEC, or the International Program on the Elimination of Child Labour—dedicated to ending child labor, particularly its worst forms. The ILO estimates that approximately 1.2 million children are in a traffic situation at any given time. Observers add that the actual number of children involved in trafficking is hard to determine because such children are often hidden from public view.

Millions of Child Laborers

Two international agreements, known as *conventions*—ILO Convention 138 and ILO Convention 182—set the guidelines for determining appropriate work for young people. Chores in a child's own home or school-related work are not child labor, according to the ILO. *Child labor* refers to work that is inappropriate because of a child's age, the nature of the work, the number of hours worked, or some combination of these factors. A job that does not interfere with school or pose harm to a child's health and well-being can be "a positive experience," says the ILO, provided it meets the legal guidelines set out by the two key labor conventions governing children.[13]

In 2006 the ILO released its latest findings on child labor. New estimates put the number of child laborers worldwide at 218 million. This is a decrease from earlier estimates of 246 million children.[14]

The ILO identifies the largest group of child laborers as living in the Asian-Pacific region. China, India, and neighboring countries are home to 122 million working children between the ages of five and fourteen. In sub-Saharan Africa, where disease

A young girl struggles with a heavy load on the outskirts of Hanoi in Vietnam. Many Vietnamese children work to help their families.

and population growth have created many social problems, roughly one child in four is trapped in child labor. By contrast, Latin America and the Caribbean are rapidly eliminating child labor and putting children in school full time.[15]

Researchers for the ILO have identified the types of work performed by children. The vast majority of children—seven out of ten—work in agriculture. Sometimes they help parents harvest crops on plantations. Others work on family farms or in small home-based businesses such as processing tobacco or harvesting cocoa pods. Agricultural work also includes hunting, fishing, and forestry jobs. Nearly one in four children works in service jobs such as washing dishes in a restaurant or cleaning rooms in a hotel. Only about 9 percent of the world's child laborers work in industrial settings such as mines or construction sites.[16]

The ILO also identifies four basic groups of cruel and unacceptable work—"the worst forms of child labor." The first is slavery: forcing someone to work. Some child camel jockeys fell into this category. Children who are trafficked for other forms of work are also in this group. For example, soldiers in some countries kidnap boys and girls and make them work in military camps. Another type of slavery is debt bondage. Children are used to pay off loans or debts for their parents. Human rights groups report that this practice continues in parts of Southeast Asia.

The second group is commercial sex work, including prostitution and pornography. Worldwide, about 1.8 million children are trapped in the commercial sex industry, according to the ILO.[17] Most of them are girls.

The third type of cruel and unacceptable child labor is illicit work. An illicit activity is one that is against the law, such as selling drugs or stealing. Roughly six hundred thousand children take part in illicit activities.[18] The largest numbers are in Asia and Latin America.

The fourth of the worst types of child labor is hazardous work. This is work that can harm the health or safety of a child. Work that damages a child's moral values is also considered harmful. Many hazardous jobs are found in agriculture, where children are exposed to dangerous chemicals or machinery. For example, harvesting sugarcane with a sharp knife called a *machete* is a form of hazardous labor. A machete can slice off fingers or toes. Climbing down a narrow mining shaft to dig out gold ore is another example. Other types of hazardous labor include polishing metal with dangerous chemicals, lifting pots of boiling glass in jewelry factories, begging on city streets, mixing chemicals for firecrackers, or breathing tobacco dust while making cigarettes.

Differing Views on Work for Children

Child labor is a complex issue. Studies reveal that most working children come from extremely poor regions. In some parts of the world, entire families live on less than a few dollars a day.

Child labor refers to work that is inappropriate because of a child's age, the nature of the work, the number of hours worked, or some combination of these factors.

Children work for many reasons. Some want to help their families survive. They may work to earn money for school fees and uniforms. Orphans often have no choice but to work. Civil wars and the HIV/AIDS virus have created millions of orphans who must take care of themselves. Crime is also a factor. Trafficking agents are known to seek out children. They may lure boys and girls from their homes with promises of education and a better life.

Many reformers say that child labor can cause physical and emotional problems. They argue that children who stay out of school are more likely to remain in poverty. Some organizations have pointed out that when child laborers eventually become parents, they may also send their children to work instead of school. A new generation will then grow up without the skills needed to earn a decent living. Research shows that society benefits financially by eliminating child labor. For every dollar spent improving the lives of children, a society stands to gain six dollars in improved productivity and better health for its citizens.[19]

However, not everyone agrees that all child labor should be abolished. For example, a group of working children in India reported in 2003 that although they did not want to work, many children desperately needed their jobs. The children said that government efforts to remove them from their jobs sometimes did more harm than good.[20]

Some members of the international community also disagree

with the minimum age limits set forth in the ILO conventions.[21] Work plays an important role in a number of cultures and may be seen as a way of preparing children for life. For centuries, children have worked alongside adults in many societies, including nineteenth-century America, where children worked in mines, factories, and stores. Today children in the United States are still allowed to work on family farms at earlier ages than the general population. These differing opinions on work for children have not been fully resolved. However, many people are hard at work to improve the lives of children.

Reformers Making a Difference

The movement to end child labor is unprecedented in size and scope, according to the ILO. A report released in 2006 shows

Two girls crush rocks at a mine near Delhi, India. Dangerous work like this is considered a cruel and unacceptable form of child labor.

that child labor is declining. In fact, if world leaders continue their efforts at the same level, the ILO says that by 2016 the worst forms of child labor will be eliminated.[22]

The International Labour Organization has been working for many years to end child labor. The ILO is an agency of the United Nations and is made up of 179 member states. Formed after World War I, the group says its mission is to seek the promotion of "social justice and internationally recognized human and labour rights."[23] The ILO develops international conventions. When member nations ratify a convention, they publicly agree to obey the guidelines. The ILO urges them to follow through on their promises and provides resources to help governments make needed changes.

The United Nations Children's Fund (UNICEF) works closely with the ILO. It was created by the United Nations after World War II. UNICEF supports child health and nutrition, good water and sanitation, education for all boys and girls, and protection of children from violence, exploitation, and AIDS. UNICEF also conducts campaigns to raise public awareness about child labor.

Another agency that plays a role in the child labor reform movement is the World Bank. The World Bank was started after World War II and is made up of 184 member countries. The World Bank seeks ways to end poverty, one of the main causes of child labor. It provides loans, grants, and other assistance to poor and developing nations.

Humanitarian groups in many countries offer aid to children. Some provide shelter, food, and training to children rescued from child labor. Others conduct research to help lawmakers better understand the problem. These organizations are known as nongovernmental organizations, or NGOs.

In September 2000, world leaders from 189 countries gathered for a special meeting at the United Nations. The meeting was called the Millennium Summit. Leaders agreed on eight goals to provide a brighter future for the world. The goals are designed to end poverty and provide every child with an education. The goals promote equality for girls and better living conditions for families. By 2015, world leaders want to reduce poverty by half. If the goals are met, reformers say, many of the root causes of child labor will be removed.

More Battles to Win

Each year UNICEF publishes a report on the health and well-being of the world's children. In 2006, UNICEF said that millions of children have not been helped, despite global progress. Child laborers are often hard to see, said the report. They work in private homes as domestic servants, on the streets, in small shops, on farms, and in countless other places.[24]

According to Ann Veneman, Executive Director of UNICEF:

> Despite efforts to improve children's lives, these are children who are being left behind. They are the exploited and abused children, and children who are subject to discrimination. They are overlooked and forgotten, by individuals, by institutions, and sometimes even by their own families.[25]

Leaders of the child labor reform movement hope to see every child receive a good education and to see sound, safe guidelines govern the working experiences of people under the age of eighteen. By all accounts, much remains to be done.

Children have always done household chores. They may wash dishes after dinner or rake leaves in the fall. Even five-year-olds can put away their toys. Such work is not child labor. In fact, some types of work may be useful. The International Labour Organization says:

> We have no problem with the little girl who helps her mother with the housework or cooking, or the boy or girl who does unpaid work in a small family business. Quite the contrary! By performing simple tasks or helping in a family enterprise, they can pick up skills.[1]

In Europe and America, "children at work" typically refers to teenagers who go to school full-time but work at part-time jobs, according to a report from the U.S. Department of Labor.[2] The report observes that most American kids get jobs to earn spending money. By contrast, student jobs in Europe often help a child learn more about a profession.[3]

How Teens Earn Money

U.S. teens who are thirteen years old and younger can baby-sit, mow lawns, or deliver newspapers to neighbors, says the U.S. Department of Labor. They can also perform in plays and movies or even become professional musicians. For example, twin sisters Mary-Kate and Ashley Olsen released their CD "Brother for Sale" in 1992, when they were six years old.

Older teens, ages fourteen to fifteen, have more opportunities to earn money. They can bag groceries, sell tickets at a summer amusement park, file papers in an office, serve hamburgers and fries, or do any other job considered "light work." However, they cannot work more than three hours on a school day. On a holiday or weekend, they cannot work more than eight hours. Jobs performed during summer vacation or school breaks must not add up to more than forty hours for the week.

Teens between the ages of sixteen and seventeen can do any job that is not hazardous. Operating a meat-cutting machine in a butcher shop is hazardous, as is washing the windows of a skyscraper. Younger teens cannot crawl into mining shafts, drive carts on airport runways, or train dangerous animals. In all, there are seventeen occupations considered unsafe for minors.

Eighteen-year-olds have no special restrictions. They are governed by the same health and safety rules that apply to adults. They can even join the military.

Different Rules on the Farm

Farm children in the United States observe different rules. If their parents own a farm, children may be involved in caring for animals and crops. Maybe they have been feeding cows or snapping green beans for as long as they can remember. They do not have to follow federal labor laws for farm workers.

Children aged twelve to thirteen can work on someone else's farm before and after school. However, they must have a parent's permission. For instance, they can harvest blueberries by hand in Oregon or remove tassels from corn in the Midwest. However, they cannot operate hay balers, feed grinders, or cotton pickers. This equipment is considered dangerous.

Many laws and practices now protect children in developed nations. This was not always so. Child labor in industrialized nations was widespread up until the early twentieth century. The U.S. Department of Labor offers a brief history of child labor in America. Historians relate that the children of early

Children worked in U.S. factories up through the early twentieth century. This little girl was photographed at work in a North Carolina mill in 1908.

settlers and colonists were expected to work. During colonial times, a type of law known as "poor laws" required children of the poor to become apprentices in the homes and businesses of wealthier people. Impoverished children as young as three were sent off to work. Later, during the Industrial Revolution, machines began doing jobs once done by people. Factories opened in Europe and later, in America, thus creating a need for cheap labor. Children took on some of these factory jobs. After the Civil War, textile mills in the Southern states created a new wave of child labor. In 1836, Massachusetts passed the first child labor law, but a national law to govern child labor did not come into being for another hundred years.[4] In England, too, children as young as four once worked in factories and mills.

A Glance at the Past

"Please, sir, I want some more." Little Oliver Twist begged for an extra bowl of soup. He was hungry after a long day in the workhouse. Instead of more food, he received a beating.

Oliver was a fictional character in a novel by Charles Dickens published in 1838. Dickens, who had worked in a factory as a child, called attention to child labor through Oliver's story.

During the middle to late 1800s, children of poor English families often worked in factories and mills. Working children served their employers six days a week. Early textile mills rarely offered fences or gates to protect workers from dangerous equipment. Factory machines had powerful, fast-moving wheels, gears, and fan belts. Stories are told of children snatched into machinery, whipped about through the gears, and crushed while horrified and helpless co-workers looked on.[5]

England was not alone. Author Ben White reports that in the Netherlands during the nineteenth century, children worked in fisheries and sugar-beet factories for up to seventeen hours per day. Children as young as four years old carried and stacked bricks in the brickyards of Moordrecht.[6] Tiny fingers could be bruised, smashed, and torn by the dried clay.

During the same period, Canadian children made boots, cigars, and clothing in Toronto and other cities. They breathed fumes in sawmills and match factories. Gangs of street children earned money by shining shoes, begging, or performing for passersby.[7]

In Nova Scotia, young boys drove pit ponies in the coal mines. They crawled through narrow underground passageways. Some miners began working by the age of eight, but most were twelve or older. Boys went to work before dawn. They spent their day in cold, black tunnels and returned home in the dark. On good days, mining work was backbreaking and dreary. On bad days, it was deadly.[8]

Explosion at Springhill

Twenty-one child miners, including a twelve-year-old, died in Springhill, Novia Scotia, when an underground explosion caused the town's coal mine to collapse.[9] Historian Robert McIntosh describes the accident:

> In the early afternoon of February 21, 1891, a charge of gunpowder was lit nineteen hundred feet underground to dislodge a small quantity of coal. The explosion backfired, igniting airborne coal dust. Wind and flame, followed by balls of fire, stormed through the entire area.[10]

An aftereffect of the explosion—a mix of smoke and poisonous gas—prevented rescue workers from reaching the miners for half an hour, explains McIntosh. When they finally arrived, they found boys and men dead beneath masses of stone and coal. Fragments of coal carts and bent iron rails were scattered about.[11] One of the only children to survive was thirteen-year-old John Conway. McIntosh writes that rescue workers followed cries of "Mother!" to a pile of debris. They found the boy buried beneath the rubble, but with no serious injuries. Another thirteen-year-old was not so lucky. Willard Carter was taken out alive, despite severe burns on his hands and face. He died before nightfall.[12]

The accident could have easily happened elsewhere. Many other countries used child miners at that time. The United States, Canada's neighbor to the south, was no exception.

Twelve-year-olds and younger children worked above ground as "breaker boys" in the anthracite coal fields of Pennsylvania, according to the U.S. Department of Labor.[13] They were often the children of poor immigrants from Italy, Ireland, or Germany. They picked rock out of piles of coal.

These breaker boys were photographed in Pittstown, Pennsylvania, in 1911. In much of the world, children still perform hazardous mining jobs.

Historical accounts describe children who spent full days stooping and bending in cold, damp surroundings. When they turned twelve, breaker boys had to go underground to work. They knew what would happen if the mining shafts collapsed, but they went anyway. Most had no choice. Their families depended on the few dollars they brought home.

Children in America's Factories

The U.S. Department of Labor estimates that by 1911, two million children were at work in American mills, canneries, factories, and shops. All were under the age of sixteen.[14] Some children worked twelve hours a day or more. Boys lifted and poured buckets of molten glass in northern glass factories. Girls labored in textile mills or in soap-packing plants where acids ate away at their fingers. Newspaper boys worked on the streets— and some of them lived there.[15]

A labor reformer observed in 1902:

> It is strange that we do nothing for our little newsboys. They are out at all hours of the night and day exposed to the most inclement weather. . . . By the time they have reached their fourteenth year they are worn out.[16]

Hard-Won Protections

Reformers began urging lawmakers to protect children. By 1913, many states had passed laws to limit the working age to fourteen years old. Laws making education compulsory through elementary school were instituted nationwide within a few years. In 1938, the federal government passed the Fair Labor Standards Act. It included guidelines for children that are still in place today, though they are not always followed.

Abuses in the Workplace

Journalist Jonathan Silvers traveled to Pakistan in the mid-1990s. He wrote an article describing the scene. Outside the main city of Lahore he saw working children everywhere. An eight-year-old boy and his younger sisters operated a fruit stand. Three boys, dressed in adult-sized uniforms, manned a gas station. A nine-year-old boy with a donkey cart ran a small delivery business.[1]

Silvers thought these sights might prepare him for his first visit to a Pakistani factory where children worked. He was wrong.

No amount of preparation could have lessened the shock and revulsion I felt on entering a sporting-goods factory in the town of Sialkot . . . where scores of children, most of them aged five to ten, produce soccer balls by hand for forty rupees, or about $1.20 a day. The children work eighty hours a week in near-total darkness and total silence.[2]

The author found appalling abuses. Sleepy or careless children went to "the back room" for punishment. There the foreman hung children upside down by their knees. Boys were beaten with either a cane or a leather strap.[3]

Silvers and others brought international attention to Pakistan's soccer ball industry. Many reforms have since taken place. In 2004, the International Labour Organization announced that Pakistan had successfully completed a program to remove children from soccer ball factories.

Reform efforts are underway throughout the world. Yet child labor abuses in the workplace continue, and not only in developing countries. Child labor can take place anywhere. Child trafficking rings operate in Europe, Japan, and the United States. Migrant farm worker children in the United States work long hours during harvest seasons, sometimes in extreme heat. Children may drop out of school to work.

Defining Child Labor

What is the difference between "children at work" and "child labor"? All children between the ages of five and eleven years old are in child labor if they work at any job *other than household chores,* says the ILO.[4] Children between the ages of twelve to fourteen are permitted to do "light work." The job cannot be hazardous. It must not require more than fourteen hours per week.

Teenagers between the ages of fifteen to seventeen can work up to forty-three hours per week. They become child laborers if they work more than forty-three hours per week. They are child laborers if they perform hazardous work or another of the worst forms of child labor.[5]

Guidelines to protect children were established in several important international agreements.

The Minimum Age Treaty

Before 1973, the ILO took steps to protect children from inappropriate work. The first convention of the ILO, in 1919, mentions the elimination of child labor but only in certain industries. Various ILO conventions set guidelines for when children should begin work in agriculture, fishing, mining, and other industries. However, countries did not have a general guideline to follow for all jobs.

In 1973, the organization adopted ILO Convention 138, also known as the Minimum Age Convention. It set a minimum age for workers across all countries and industries. ILO Convention 138 went into force on June 19, 1976. The new agreement replaced earlier ones.

ILO Convention 138 establishes fifteen years old as the general age to start work. Children in developing nations can go to work sooner. However, they must have first completed compulsory schooling. The convention also lays out guidelines for "light work." It protects children from excessive hours and hazardous conditions.

Unacceptable Activities for Children

In June of 1999, the ILO voted to adopt a sweeping new measure. Some forms of child labor were so dangerous or otherwise harmful that they must be stopped immediately, the ILO said. Countries must remove children from unacceptable forms of work, provide free basic education, and help young people rebuild their lives.

The new agreement was called the Worst Forms of Child Labor Convention or ILO Convention 182. It greatly expanded protections for children. The new agreement urged nations to remove children from four categories of work:

- *Slavery and all forms of work that resemble slavery.* These include the trafficking and sale of children, debt bondage, and forced labor. One type of forced labor specifically forbidden is the use of child soldiers.

- *Commercial sex work.* Children in prostitution and pornography compose the second group.

- *Illicit activities.* These include producing or selling drugs. Children are sometimes involved in trafficking schemes where they help adults locate or lure other children.

- *Hazardous work.* Any work that "by its nature or the circumstances in which it is carried out, is likely to harm the health, safety or morals of children" meets the definition of the worst form of child labor.[6]

The last category covers the largest group of children. The ILO reports that nearly two thirds of all child laborers perform hazardous work. Hazardous jobs range from mining and construction work to deep-sea diving. Even farm work contains many hazards, such as pesticides and dangerous machinery. In the United States alone, thousands of children are injured each year from accidents involving farm equipment.

ILO Convention 182 asks countries to monitor working conditions. Governments are urged to design programs to reach children at risk. World leaders are asked to consider the special needs of girls, who often face discrimination based on gender in many countries.

Children Have Human Rights

Another important agreement that protects boys and girls from child labor is the Convention on the Rights of the Child (CRC). World leaders signed it on November 20, 1989.

Children crush bricks in Dhaka, Bangladesh. Most of those engaged in the worst forms of child labor are doing hazardous work.

Provisions went into effect in the fall of 1990. Nearly every country in the world has ratified the CRC. (Ratification indicates formal approval; however, there is no legal mechanism to force the ratifying countries to obey its terms.)

Children have the right to live in freedom and dignity, according to the CRC. The agreement calls for schooling and the opportunity to grow and develop during childhood. It says that children should not do inappropriate, dangerous, or illegal work.

Seven key provisions deal with child labor. Article 28 says that every child has the right to an education. Article 31 defends the rights of children to play, relax, and pursue enriching activities such as art and music. Article 32 protects children from dangerous work, long hours, unfair pay, and activities that harm health and happiness. Article 33 protects children from the drug trade and Article 34 from the commercial sex industry. Article 35 bans trafficking and other forms of slavery such as bonded labor. Children should not become soldiers nor be forced to work in military camps, says Article 38. It forbids military groups from recruiting children under the age of fifteen.[7]

UNICEF and the Seven Types of Child Labor

Today—even with two international labor conventions in place to protect children and widespread ratification of the CRC— abuses still occur in the workplace. Unfortunately, there is no way to enforce the ILO conventions. Government leaders must voluntarily put the provisions into action at the national level.

UNICEF identified seven types of children's labor in 1997. The first six were "domestic service, forced and bonded labor, commercial sexual exploitation, industrial and plantation work, street work, and work for the family."[8]

Girls often suffer from gender discrimination in the home and in the workplace. If a family can afford to send only one child to school, for example, parents might send their son instead of their daughter. Girls also work longer hours and are more likely to suffer sexual exploitation. "Girls' work" therefore made up the seventh type of labor.

Today UNICEF does not use the seven categories to describe child labor. It speaks more simply about the hardships of children who suffer from poverty, lack of health care, and basic education. These children include those trapped in hazardous work and in the worst forms of child labor. UNICEF strongly supports the Millennium Development Goals as a way to help end the suffering of disadvantaged children.[9]

Invisible Servants. They work in private homes, often isolated from their families and peers. No one monitors their

Micheline never knew her father—he was assassinated before she was old enough to remember him. But she does remember her mother. When Micheline was a small child in Haiti, her mother left her one evening in a deserted area and told her to wait for her aunt to come and get her. No one ever came. After a terrifying night in the jungle, hearing the sounds of wild animals, Micheline made her way to the house of someone she knew. She poured out her story. "So the next morning, they brought me to my aunt, and that's when my whole awful childhood began."

Micheline never saw her mother again. She later learned that her mother had died. Her aunt and uncle moved into her home. Micheline was forced to become a servant. "I had to wake up early in the morning, get water for them to shower, take care of the chickens, feed the animals, clean the house, do laundry . . . just a never-ending story." Her cousin and uncle frequently beat her.

Eventually Micheline was sent to Connecticut to live with another cousin. When she arrived in the United States, she learned that her cousin had purchased her for $2,500 to take care of three children, including a newborn baby. Micheline was also expected to do all of the housework.

"I cried for months and months and months," recalls Micheline, who was overwhelmed by the responsibility of feeding, washing, and dressing three small children. "I was the one waking up in the middle of the night with the baby." She had to feed the baby and take care of it. "I had no sleep whatsoever." Her cousin was never satisfied with Micheline's performance. "Nothing was ever good enough. I never finished anything on time. I never did anything right." Micheline was accused of being ungrateful for her "opportunity" to be in America. As before, she received beatings from her cousin.

The emotional torment of her childhood is what she remembers as the hardest part about being a child servant. "I had no childhood. I don't know what it is like to be a child . . . to have peace, and feel safe, and to feel wanted, to feel love." Her cousin's cruelty made her life especially difficult. "When someone makes you feel like you are worthless, there is nothing that can compensate for that. . . . It requires a miracle to actually pull through it."

A friend could have done much to make her life easier during those years of working for her cousin. When she arrived in Connecticut, Micheline was old enough to attend seventh grade. Her cousin allowed her to go to a local school, but Micheline was unable to make friends. Part of the problem was that she spoke little English. The other students ignored her. It may have been the fact that she was always sad that drove away the other children, or that she dressed differently. "I didn't have nice clothes. I was just a lost child. I don't blame them, I just wish that some of them would be friendly." Even a smile would have been enough to brighten her day.

In her late teenage years, Micheline found the courage to run away from her cousin. She found a place to live with a neighbor while she attended secretarial school. Eventually Micheline was able to get a good job and a house of her own.

Today she loves to daydream about returning to her village to help the little *restavecs*, as child domestic servants are called in Haiti. In her dreams she would enter private homes and rescue every child living in unpaid servitude. "Take each and every one of them and fill them with . . . everything I never had."[10]

working conditions. In fact, members of the public rarely know anything about the millions of girls who work as domestic servants. Most are between the ages of twelve and seventeen.[11] The ILO says that girls working as domestic servants account for the single largest group of child workers in the world.[12] They live in Southeast Asia, Africa, Latin America and other areas.

Reports from UNICEF, the ILO, and other organizations reveal that domestic servants work long hours for very little pay. In fact, some children are not paid at all. A typical worker will cook meals, wash the laundry, polish the floors, shop for supplies, run errands, and take care of children.

When does a domestic servant get to talk to friends, take a walk, or go to a party? Many girls in an African study said "Never." They did not get rest breaks, free weekends, or time off for holidays.[13]

The report pointed out that not all domestic workers are live-ins, nor are they all girls. Some boys and girls live at home and go to work during the day. Their jobs are better than those of children who live with their employers. Children who live in their own homes are more likely to have time in the evening to see friends and family members. However, many domestic workers do not have time to go to school.

The ILO reports that nearly two thirds of all child laborers perform hazardous work—work "likely to harm the health, safety or morals of children."

Boys and girls interviewed by humanitarian groups often complain of verbal abuse by employers. Domestic servants receive insults when they make mistakes or work too slowly. Sometimes they are beaten or even sexually abused.

"I don't like the job, I get very tired every night and I cry to sleep, but there is nowhere I can get money from, I am forced to work," said a thirteen-year-old domestic servant in Lusaka, Zambia, Africa.[14]

Millions of other servants feel the same. They are trapped, frightened, and depressed. Most have dropped out of school because of family poverty. Without training or job skills they have nowhere else to go.

Bearing the Burden of Debt.
Nearly 5.7 million children work in forced or bonded labor.[15] Bonded labor—also called debt bondage—is a system under which a person who cannot pay off a debt works for the person they owe or sends a family member to work. Debt bondage takes place in several areas of the world. It has long been a problem in Asia, particularly in India, Pakistan, and Nepal. In 1997, UNICEF explained how debt bondage worked in India's carpet district. Poor families sometimes accepted small loans from factory owners. Children were then "bonded" or given to the factory to pay off the debt.[16] Children might be paid so little that years of work fail to remove the debt.

Generations of families in Nepal have participated in a form of bonded agricultural work known as the *kamaiyas* system. Families worked to pay off debts created by their ancestors. A child labor study conducted in 2001 described some of the hardships for children. Three fourths of the children worked twelve hours a day or more, often beginning as early as 4:00 A.M. Girls typically cleaned the kitchen, fed the farm animals, and took care of small children. Some would also help in the rice fields. Boys were most often used to herd cattle and goats. Children in the study rarely had time to attend school. Nearly one third of the children interviewed said they worked to help pay off their parents' debts to the landowners. Kamaiyas was declared illegal in 2000, and more than thirty thousand children were set free by law. However, at the time of the study, researchers found many children still working to help pay off family loans.[17]

Bonded agricultural labor is reported in other countries, too.

Young farmworkers in India in the fields. Agricultural work is the most common form of child labor.

A fourteen-year-old boy in rural India described his life as a bonded servant:

> I live in the house of my landlord, who owns 22 acres of land. I live in his house 24 hours a day. I work during the day in the fields. I scatter manure in the fields, fetch water from the well, graze cattle, give them fodder, bathe them in the pond, wash utensils, water the garden in the house of my landlord. I don't get paid any wage for this work. Only food.[18]

At the time of the interview, the boy had been working for four years. He wanted to learn a trade such as carpentry or tailoring. He had often begged his master to allow him to leave. His employer refused.

Girls at Risk. More than one million children are thought to be trapped in the commercial sex trade, according to the U.S. State Department.[19] Most are girls. In 2000, the ILO estimated that 590,000 preteen and teenage girls were working in the sex industry in Asia alone.[20]

Many children are moved by traffickers and forced to become prostitutes. However, trafficking is not always part of the problem. Wars as well as the HIV/AIDS epidemic have left millions of children without one or both parents. Orphans may turn to prostitution because they have no other way to make a living.

At Work in Fields and Factories. Agricultural activities account for 70 percent of all child labor worldwide.[21] Children work on family farms, commercial farms, and plantations. They plant, weed, and harvest coffee, tea, sugarcane, rubber, bananas, cocoa, cotton, tobacco and other products. Boys and girls work long hours in the hot sun. Daily life includes exposure to pesticides, equipment with sharp blades and moving parts, snakes and insects, and poor sanitation.

A smaller percentage of children work in factories and sweatshops. A sweatshop is a business that often ignores labor laws and health and safety regulations. For example, fire exits may be blocked, machines may operate without protective guards, or the building may have faulty floors and ceilings. Workers will typically be paid very little in exchange for many hours of work. Sweatshop owners may try to avoid paying taxes.[22]

Life on the Streets

Foreign visitors were disturbed by the thousands of children who roamed the streets of Phnom Penh in Cambodia. Some

As a child, Eulogio Alejandre knew hunger. Sometimes, when food was scarce, his mother would cook a small pot of beans for him and his nine siblings. "My mom would say, 'Here's your portion,' and that was it. We couldn't ask for more because there was no more." At such times he would go to bed dreaming of beans and fruit everywhere. But when he woke up there was no food. He remembers days and weeks of feeling empty.

When Eulogio was thirteen, his father gathered the family together and they slipped over the border that divides Mexico from Arizona. The family entered "in the middle of the night, unwelcomed, into the United States." They traveled hundreds of miles more to settle in Utah. Soon Eulogio began working as a child laborer in the cherry orchards. His day began at five in the morning during the summer months when the ground was still wet with dew. The family worked until midday, then took a break. In the afternoon they returned and worked until dark.

He was grateful for the work. If the hours were long and tiring, he didn't mind because he could always climb down from the branches, lean against the tree, and eat as many cherries as he wanted—just like in his dreams. When the weather was bad, he was thankful to live in a house that did not leak.

Eulogio worked in the tree tops, walking from branch to branch. He usually slung one bucket around his neck and strapped another to his waist. He recalls scampering like a monkey through the trees, "just picking cherries and letting them fall into the bucket." If a branch broke under his foot, he was quick to grab onto the branch overhead to keep from falling.

Eulogio never hurt himself. However, a visiting friend was not so lucky. The friend lost his balance, slid down the tree, and was stabbed by a branch. The friend was rushed to the emergency room. Eulogio remembers life in the orchards as a stream of "constant injuries" for the workers. Children frequently fell off tractors, breaking arms or legs when they hit the ground. Sometimes buckets fell from the trees and hit a child in the head or landed on someone's leg. "It was to be expected and we did the best we could to protect ourselves," he says.

Another hazard was pesticides, though Eulogio did not understand the threat at the time. The cherries he loved were often covered with a white film. Even if he had known he was supposed to wash the cherries before eating them, the only water available was a stream that ran through the orchard. Pesticides from the trees had probably made their way into the water. (Later in life, as an adult, Eulogio witnessed the seriousness of exposure to pesticides. A child in Utah was accidentally sprayed with pesticides and did not understand the need to wash off the spray. The child died the following day.)

As he grew older, Eulogio began to tire of days in the fields. He didn't want to spend his entire life picking fruit or onions. Yes, the days were hot and the buckets heavy, but that wasn't the real problem. The worst thing about being a child laborer in the fields was the feeling that his opportunities were slipping away. The hardest thing was "the mental anguish of not seeing better things."

A new dream began to take shape: He wanted to become a teacher. Impossible, said his father. "Look here, you need to just work hard, save money, because why would they give a job to an illegal alien rather than a white citizen?" His father told him to save his money, work hard in the orchards in the summers, maybe get a good job at the local trucking company, and to quit wasting his time thinking about such things as being a teacher.

Eulogio refused to listen. He saw that the bridge out of poverty was education. "So I did everything possible to educate myself. I would pick up a newspaper, translate the articles in the newspaper, just for my own benefit. . . . I would watch television . . . the news, CNN, and become knowledgeable about the world. I would read on my own. . . . If the teacher said, 'You're going to read twenty pages today,' I would read one hundred pages."

In time, Eulogio Alejandre achieved his goal. He became a U.S. citizen, a teacher, and then the principal of a high school. He looks back on his childhood experiences with mixed feelings. "I am glad I had the opportunity to work in the fields, but under no circumstances would I want my children or any other children to have to work in the fields," he says. His greatest reward as an adult has been to see students from migrant families learn to have faith in themselves. "It is amazing the number of students from the high school where I work who have decided to go to college in the last four years." Even though Alejandre has had the opportunity to take higher paying work in the business world, he loves education. He says, "There's no paycheck in the world that can compensate my efforts in helping these kids."[23]

street children sold vegetables; others begged for food. The governor decided they were "an eyesore" to tourists.

In June 2003 police herded the children into vehicles and transported them out of the city. False news reports claimed the children were going to a drug rehabilitation center in Banteay Meanchey Province. The children never arrived. They were dropped off on the side of the road beyond the city limits. While many eventually made their way back to the city, some were never found.[24]

Street children are found in many towns and cities throughout the developing world. They sell small items, shine shoes, and guard parked cars to survive. Some beg for a living, such as members of well-organized gangs in several Thai cities.

Life on the street is dangerous. Children often face physical threats from older children, merchants, and sometimes from local police. Thieves may try to take their meager earnings. Studies have shown that while most children go home at night, taking their money to their families, others live full-time on the streets. Some—even in developed countries such as the United States—are described as "throwaway children," because their families will no longer take care of them.

When Work Interferes With School

According to UNICEF, the most common type of work for children is family work at home and on family farms.[25] Often boys and girls do different tasks. Girls help their mothers cook, clean, and wash clothes. Boys, particularly older ones, help their fathers in the fields or in family workshops. Both boys and girls may care for animals, tend family gardens, and harvest crops.

Family work can have some benefits: helping the family, teaching responsibility and skills, and giving children a sense of pride. However, UNICEF says, family work is not always beneficial. Hours may be too long or the work too difficult for growing children. Work that keeps a child out of school is also a problem.

Girls at Work

Girls are often overworked, and their efforts are often unappreciated. Some families do not allow girls to go to school. These are a few of the reasons why UNICEF treats girls' work as a special category.

Girls throughout the world often work longer hours than boys, according to UNICEF. Sociology professor Loretta Bass, who studied child labor in Africa, illustrates this point with the story of Zvaipa, a thirteen-year-old in Zambia. Zvaipa resented her heavy workload.

> Today I went to wash plates in the morning. Before I even left for school and after I had dried the plates, I started grinding sorghum. When I came from school I cooked sadza for my brothers and myself. After eating I went to wash plates again. When I came from washing plates I went to grind.[26]

One Sunday Zvaipa refused to wash plates. Her mother beat her. "After beating me she told me to go and wash them. After that mother did not beat me at all."[27]

Zvaipa's brother had a different life. He worked for three hours in the fields and then went to play with his friends for the afternoon. No one expected him to serve his siblings as well as the adults.

Henrietta Abane, a lecturer in sociology at the University of Cape Coast in Ghana, wrote an article about the attitudes of local parents toward their daughters. The article cites a revealing study. An NGO conducted a workshop in a community in southern Ghana to help parents see that they treated boys and girls differently. At the beginning of the workshop, parents said that they did not think girls were hardworking students. Then the NGO had the parents take a closer look at how their children used their time. The demonstration made it clear that girls

A twelve-year-old girl carries firewood at a brick factory in Kabul, Afghanistan. Children at the factory can take home free firewood for their homes. Many children all over the world work to help their families.

began their day around 5:00 A.M. by cleaning the house and ended their day around 10:00 P.M. after washing the dishes. At the end, the parents decided that the problem was not "girls are not learning hard enough" but was "girls are working too hard."[28]

Exhaustion and overwork are not the only challenges for girls. There are other pressures, too. Employers may try to force them into sexual activities, says UNICEF. Girls in some societies are viewed as less important than boys. For example, in India when women marry, they belong to their husband's family, so their training or schooling and their work efforts do not benefit their birth family. Parents may not see the benefits of sending a girl to school. A mother from India explained her view:

> Why should I waste my time and money on sending my daughter to school where she will learn nothing of use? . . . Too much schooling will only give girls big ideas.[29]

Child Labor Abuses in the United States

A study conducted in 2000 found that 148,000 children and youth are employed illegally in an average week in the United States. The minors work too many hours or in hazardous occupations. The study also pointed out other important health and safety concerns.[30]

Child prostitution is another serious problem in the United States. In fact, "It is the nation's least recognized epidemic," says Richard J. Estes, a professor at the University of Pennsylvania. Runaways, street children, and trafficked children are at risk. Many street children turn to drugs "to deal with the emotional pain of being . . . sexually victimized," says Estes.[31]

Trafficking occurs in the United States, as in other industrialized nations. Children are trafficked from Central and Eastern Europe and other countries to work as domestic servants and prostitutes. Estes says that children from Africa, Asia, Eastern Europe and Latin America enter the country illegally to work in child prostitution.[32]

One analyst estimates that forty-five thousand to fifty thousand women and children are brought to the U. S. each year by "small crime rings." Criminal gangs smuggle children into the country and force them to work. Powerful captors guard the children, forcing them to live as slaves.[33]

4

Trapped in Slave Labor

A slave is owned or controlled by another person. Some types of child labor are so oppressive that they amount to slavery. Children cannot quit their jobs. They are not free to miss work if they are sick. They cannot refuse to do their assigned job, even if the work is painful, frightening, or dangerous.

ILO Convention 182 identifies several modern forms of slavery. One type of slavery involves the sale and trafficking of children. Another type is debt bondage, an ancient practice. Debt bondage continues today, even though it is against the law. Forced labor is also slavery. A 2005 report found 12.3 million people forced to work in a variety of industries, including farming, manufacturing, and prostitution. The ILO estimates that between 4 and 6 million of these workers are children.[1] Child soldiers are another example of forced labor.

Soldiers Came to School

Imagine going to class with nothing on your mind except your math homework. Then, soldiers arrive. They have guns and knives. They burn your school. Then they herd you off to a dirty campsite. You will live with them for a long time. You don't know how long. You don't know if you will ever see your parents again.

In 2001 this nightmarish scenario happened in Burundi. Rebel soldiers arrived at a boarding school in Bujumbura. Soldiers burned down the library, the dormitory, and the director's office before kidnapping more than two hundred boys.[2]

Four boys escaped, including Policarp Ntakarutimana. He told reporters:

> They told us we had to follow them, because they too had abandoned school to join the rebellion. . . . We were approaching some hills when the military started shooting. The rebels were shooting back, and I used this to run away because I was afraid.[3]

Since the 1960s, civil wars have rocked Nigeria, Ethiopia, Sudan, Liberia, Sierra Leone, Somalia, Rwanda and the Democratic Republic of the Congo.[4] Communities have been destroyed. Many children have become orphans. Worse still, soldiers who kill the parents often kidnap the children.

Once inside the rebel camp, boys do a variety of tasks. They carry equipment and run messages behind enemy lines. They learn to use deadly weapons. Girls are also kidnapped by soldiers. Sometimes girls are trained to fight, but more often they cook and clean for the men. Soldiers often force girls to become their wives.

Child soldiers told their stories at an international conference in 2003. A girl named Emilia described life in a rebel camp. She was one of the lucky few who managed to escape.

Emilia's Story

Emilia lived near a mining district in the southern part of Sierra Leone. Rebels attacked her village in 1994. A soldier shot her brother and ordered Emilia to help bury him outside of town. She was only nine years old.

She managed to escape with her mother and several other people into the open fields near her village. Emilia and her mother hid for six months. They nearly starved. One day Emilia went to hunt for food. Rebel soldiers found her. They took her to their camp, where she joined other prisoners. The captives were "treated like slaves," Emilia recalls. "They beat us like any other animal. In fact, some were killed."[5]

She lived in the jungle for five years with the soldiers. One of her jobs was to look for food. They also taught her to set traps for the enemy. She carried heavy loads from one campsite to the next. "Sometimes our feet got swelled up because of walking on the route," she said.[6]

The commander of the group forced Emilia to become his wife. When he was killed in a battle, she finally escaped. She was fourteen years old.

Emilia was able to rebuild her life. A missionary group helped her go back to school. She was also reunited with her younger brother, the only member of her family still living. Although countries throughout Africa have made progress towards resolving conflicts, many children are still trapped in military camps.

Conflicts Continue

During the 1990s, more than two million children died as a result of armed conflicts; over one million have been made orphans; over six million have been seriously injured or disabled; and over 10 million have been left with grave psychological trauma.[7]

Many wars are winding down in Africa. Years of fighting are

In Sierra Leone, a boy with a rifle lines up with other child soldiers. During recent African civil wars, many children were forced to fight.

drawing to a close in Angola, Sierra Leone, Liberia, Angola, and the Democratic Republic of the Congo. Military groups have freed thousands of children. However, up to one hundred thousand African children are still trapped in conflict, says the Coalition to Stop the Use of Child Soldiers.[8] Researchers in 2004 found child soldiers in Uganda and other countries.

Although fighting has lessened in northern Uganda, boys and girls are still at risk from the Lord's Resistance Army (LRA).[9] The LRA has terrorized children for decades, forcing many to become "night commuters."

Night Commuters

After supper they waved goodbye. Hundreds of Ugandan children then left their refugee camps and walked to a safer town to spend the night. They were running away from the Lord's Resistance Army—and with good reason. During the last nineteen years, LRA soldiers have captured twenty-five thousand children, both boys and girls.[10]

"Jimmy" (not his real name) was fourteen when he was captured, but he later escaped. He told reporters in 2005 about the people who abused him. Some had themselves been abducted as children:

> I heard one say he would remain a fighter because he wanted to abduct children just like it happened to him, and torture them as payback for all that he went through when he, too, was abducted.[11]

Why do soldiers want children? One reason is to replenish fighters. Modern lightweight weapons make it possible for a ten-year-old to take part in combat, says Olara A. Otunnu, former UN Special Representative for Children and Armed Conflict.[12]

Most child soldiers are between the ages of ten to fifteen, but some are as young as seven.[13] Children are easy to control and useful to military groups. They carry weapons for soldiers, travel into towns to spy, and stand guard while soldiers sleep.

In 2003, Otunnu described the size of the problem to a group of world leaders. Otunnu explained that children continue to suffer after they are rescued. They have emotional scars. They are unable to forget the cruelty they have witnessed or perhaps have been forced to commit. Many find it difficult to fit back into society, he said.

Nearly half of the world's child soldiers are in sub-Saharan Africa, but young people also fight in Asia and Latin America. Roughly three hundred thousand children work as soldiers in thirty countries throughout the world.[14]

Children also fight in India, Indonesia, Nepal, and Sri Lanka. A nine-year-old boy in Myanmar (formerly Burma) told how he was pulled out of his home:

> A group of soldiers knocked loudly on the door. Five others, all about the same age, did not escape and were taken by the soldiers.

I was crying. I was dragged out of my house and put on a boat and taken to Rangoon.[15]

Children in Cambodia were recruited and forced to transport explosives for the commander and his men. One child said:

We were terrified of landmines. The paths up the mountain were littered with them. It was difficult to concentrate both on carrying huge shells and watching out for landmines.[16]

The area wars for which children are recruited are typically conflicts between religious or ethnic groups, says UNICEF. It reports that most child soldiers are forced to join military groups. However, not all child soldiers are forced. Some boys and girls agree to fight to defend their families. Some say they have become soldiers for a cause, such as fighting oppression against their religion or culture.[17]

Berta, a child from El Salvador, told her story in 2003. She grew up in a poor family near Santiago. By the time she was five years old she was in the fields helping her parents pick coffee beans. She explained that during the 1970s, people in El Salvador had organized protest movements to improve conditions for poor working people. Eventually the protesters began fighting with the government. Rebel soldiers, also called guerillas, lived and fought near Berta's home.

They would use the children to make us go to the store to get stuff for them. Also, they would use us to take the food that our parents had been forced to cook for them. In 1990, I decided to join, to help build a true democracy. I wanted life to be different in my country. I wanted life to be different for my children.[18]

Berta was fourteen years old when she joined the guerillas. The soldiers trained her to operate radar equipment. Her job was to protect the base. After one year of working for the rebels, she was shot in the back. Rescuers from the International Red Cross took her to a hospital where Berta spent two years in a wheelchair. She finally learned to walk again using crutches.

Soldiers Are Like Slaves

Children who take part in armed combat live in conditions that resemble slavery. Once a child becomes part of a military group—even if the child agreed to join—the young person is no longer free. Those who try to leave will be punished or killed. Every day is filled with danger, often violence and cruelty. Living conditions threaten their health and human dignity. Many do not survive.

Whether children want to fight or not, armed conflict violates international safeguards for children. It is one of the unconditional worst forms of child labor. Many countries, such as Burundi, are ending their civil wars. Efforts are under way to rescue children still left in camps. The job ahead is to help those children rebuild their lives.

Child soldiers in Myanmar (formerly Burma) perform drills. Many of those who escape from military groups find it hard to resume normal lives.

Trafficking

Traffickers move a person from one place to another in order to perform work at a new destination. Sometimes victims are lured or deceived into thinking that a good job or a promising education is waiting for them. Once the victim is delivered to the new employer, the trafficked person is forced to work. Agents may take a boy or girl to another country or simply to a stone quarry outside the child's home city, says the U.S. State Department. In both cases, the agent makes a profit.[19]

More than a million children per year are trafficked throughout the world. Both boys and girls are at risk. The ILO reports that boys tend to be trafficked to work on commercial farms or to do illegal work such as stealing or selling drugs. Girls are put to work as domestic servants or prostitutes.[20]

Trafficking patterns vary from region to region. In Asia, children are trafficked in Bangladesh, Nepal, Sri Lanka, Pakistan, Indonesia, Thailand, Cambodia, and China. In some Thai cities, for example, orphans and small children are trafficked from Myanmar and Cambodia and put on the streets to beg. Children are used in the drug trade. Boys trafficked to Thailand delivered drugs for warlords in Bangkok. Drug dealers want boys because they are easy to control, explains the U.S. State Department. If arrested, a boy spends less time in jail than an adult.[21]

Children are trafficked to and from many African countries. Anti-Slavery International studied children trafficked between Benin and Gabon. One young girl, who was eventually rescued, described a day she received a beating from her employer:

> I couldn't sell a lot of fruit that day. I went back home and my "auntie" beat me because I didn't bring enough money. I ran away to cry behind the house. . . . One day, I fled by going through the forest until Libreville. From there I was brought back to Benin.[22]

Trafficking is a worldwide problem. It is often linked to

sexual abuse. UNICEF reports that in all countries, most trafficked children are forced into the commercial sex trade.[23]

The Commercial Sex Industry and Slavery

It happens like this, says the U.S. State Department. A fifteen-year-old girl in Amsterdam meets a boy from Morocco. He buys her nice things and convinces her to go away with him. They move to another city. Life is wonderful at first but things start to change. One day he brings home strange men. Soon he forces her to become a prostitute.[24]

A young girl in Cambodia is promised a good job in Malaysia as a household servant. Her sponsor arranges all the papers. Once the girl arrives in Malaysia, her passport is taken away. Her sponsor disappears. She meets her real employer—the owner of a club. She is forced to dance for customers.[25]

Agents who work in the commercial sex trade often deceive their victims. Consider the story of Viola (not her real name), which appeared in a 2005 report on trafficking published by the U.S. State Department:

> Viola, a young Albanian, was 13 when she started dating 21-year-old Dilin, who proposed to marry her, then move to Italy where he had cousins who could get him a job. Arriving in Italy, Viola's life changed forever. Dilin locked her in a hotel room and left her, never to be seen again. A group of men entered and began to beat Viola.[26]

The men later forced her to become a prostitute. Dilin was a trafficking agent. He lured Viola with the promise of marriage. Agents sometimes promise girls good jobs in another city. A small advance against earnings may be given to the girl or to her parents. Too late she discovers that her new job will be prostitution.

Although most victims are girls, boys are also trafficked for commercial sex. While the problem occurs in all regions of the world, most child sex work is concentrated in Latin America, the Asian Pacific region, and developed countries.[27] The ILO says as many as 1.8 million children between the ages of five and seventeen are involved.

Child trafficking for the commercial sex industry is a serious problem in Thailand. One estimate said that forty thousand child prostitutes were at work in Thailand in 2004. The country is a place where children arrive from other destinations and is also a source of child labor. Agents bring girls as young as twelve years old from Myanmar, China, and Laos to work as prostitutes, and Thai children are sent to other countries to work.[28]

> **Some types of child labor are so oppressive that they amount to slavery. Children cannot refuse to do their assigned work, even if the job is painful, frightening, or dangerous.**

Thailand is one of the countries where child sex tourism is on the rise. Child sex tourism—in which tourists travel to other countries to find child prostitutes—is a growing problem worldwide, says the U.S. State Department. Tourists may believe that foreign laws will be more lenient than laws in their home country. Agents and customers take advantage of children from poor families. They may bribe officials so the crime will not be reported or prosecuted. The Internet makes it possible for agents and tourists to make secret arrangements and swap pictures. "The crime is typically fueled by weak law enforcement, corruption, the Internet, ease of travel, and poverty," reports the U.S. State Department.[29] During the last five years, many countries have established stiffer penalties for sex tourists. Thirty-two nations have new laws in place to discourage this practice.

Bonded Labor: A Form of Slavery

What smells worse than a can of sardines? Try three thousand cans. That's how many tin containers fourteen-year-old Jacqueline filled per day at a sardine factory in the Philippines.

This child in Zimbabwe is carrying mud bricks to a construction site.
Children who do not work fast enough are often beaten.

Jacqueline worked and lived at the factory for three years during the mid-1990s. Work began at 3:00 A.M. and lasted twelve hours a day. During shifts she often sliced her fingers on sharp metal and fish bones. Constant exposure to the pickling brine caused her hands to wrinkle.[30] Her story appeared in an ILO publication to show how children and their families are trapped by debts into slave-like jobs.

Jacqueline was put to work by an employment agency that charged her 16,000 pesos (almost $1,500 at 2007 rates) in exchange for finding her a job. Her employer at the sardine factory added new charges each day for food. In fact, her daily charges added up to more than her daily pay. In this way the factory owner was able to increase Jacqueline's debt. Locked in her room at night, forbidden to speak to outsiders, she was a prisoner. At last a child protection group rescued her.[31]

Schemes like the one that trapped Jacqueline are a form of slavery. Sometimes neither the parents who received the loan nor the child understand the size of the debt or how it will be paid off, says the U.S. State Department. Parents may not be able to read or write. They do not understand the terms of the agreement.

Dishonest employers take advantage of the situation. Some add new expenses to keep the debt in place. They may charge the child for supplies, training, food, mistakes, or any number of items. Like Jacqueline, children can work for years and still not be able to repay the money.

Slavery must be eliminated as quickly as possible, according to ILO Convention 182. No matter the form—trafficking, bonded labor, or forced labor—slavery is a violation of children's rights.

At Work in the Informal Economy

Developing nations in Asia and Africa are home to most of the world's child laborers. The ILO estimates that 122 million children between the ages of five and fourteen work in Asia and the region known as the Pacific Rim. These nations include China, India, Pakistan, Thailand, Sri Lanka, Bangladesh, and the sunny islands of Indonesia.[1]

Sub-Saharan Africa has about 50 million children who work. Compared to the overall population, this number is very high. It means that one out of every four children is at work.[2]

Less than 5 percent of children aged five to fourteen are at work in Latin America and the Caribbean.[3] Great Britain the United States, Japan, and other developed nations have the fewest numbers of all. Less than one percent of child laborers live in industrialized nations.[4] However, child labor takes place in every region of the world.

Who are the children involved in child labor? What do they do? Where do they work?

Not in Banks or Computer Stores

A newspaper article in 2006 captured the plight of seven-year-old Karen and her parents, who live near Buenos Aires in Argentina. Karen and her family climb aboard a train every night and travel to the city. When they arrive, they search through bags of garbage for plastic bottles, boxes and tin cans. Like many of Argentina's unemployed families, they are scavengers. Some people call them "ragpickers." They hunt for used items to sell at a recycling center.[5] Children in many parts of the world have similar stories.

Government studies describe life at a dump site in El Salvador, where young workers divide jobs by age. Younger boys and girls guard glass bottles and plastic jugs against rival workers. Older children in search of new treasures crawl over rat-infested mountains of paper bags, broken glass, rotting food, and empty containers.[6]

Tanzania's young scavengers sometimes work in bare feet. A street child living at a dump site in Dar Es Salaam described his life. He did not like working in the dump, but he had to take care of his brothers and sisters. "The dump has a very strong and choking smell," he said. "But I have only two alternatives: . . . either become a thief . . . or continue scavenging."[7]

Scavenging does not require special skills. Anyone can hunt for bottles and cans. Whole families often work together. No one needs a license or special permit from the government. This type of work takes place in the *informal economy*. Informal work and the people who perform it often fall outside the realm of labor laws that govern banks, stores, and factories. In the formal marketplace, owners are supposed to obey health and safety regulations. Employees need basic skills. Many workers have training in finance, computer science, or some other field.

Informal Work for Families

Experts say that the informal economy is where most child workers are found.[8] These children typically help their families, often without pay. For example, children might weave carpet on a loom in their home, stitch garments in a corner of the living room, or paint rattan furniture in a shed behind the house. They help out in family restaurants. If work for the family requires so many hours that a child cannot attend school, then the work is unacceptable according to international labor treaties.

The informal economy includes domestic service and street work. However, most child workers—seven out of ten—are found in agriculture.[9] Fishing and forestry are also part of agricultural work.

Most Work in Agriculture

Crops and practices vary from region to region, but hazards are commonplace in agriculture. Farm work can be dangerous. Fatal accidents on the job are twice as likely to happen in agriculture as in other occupations.[10] One reason involves equipment and tools. Farm children may use knives and machetes to harvest crops like sugarcane, cocoa pods, and sisal. They may work near dangerous machinery. There are other dangers, too. Pesticides sprayed on plants can get into the lungs. Snakes may be hiding behind rows of plants. Children spend long hours in the fields.

Too much work interferes with children's education. Children worry, too. An eight-year old girl working in the hybrid cottonseed fields of Andhra Pradesh, India, told

A boy scavenges through trash in Islamabad, Pakistan. Many children work as ragpickers, looking for items to sell at recycling centers.

researchers how she felt: "Whenever I see children of my age who are going to school, I get a feeling that I am missing something and feel bad about myself," the girl said.[11]

Activists investigating her worksite found unsafe conditions. Pesticides sprayed on the plants created dangerous fumes. Other child workers complained of headaches and burning eyes. Some kids fainted after fields were sprayed. They did not wear masks or gloves for protection.[12] And young workers were poorly paid for facing such risks: They received 18 rupees for twelve hours of work. That amounts to roughly 41 cents.[13]

Most children who work are in the informal economy, helping their families. Often they do not get paid.

A world away, migrant farm children from Haiti work alongside adults in the sugar fields of the Dominican Republic. A boy interviewed in 2006 told reporters about his life. He lives in a shanty with no running water or electricity. He has been harvesting sugarcane since the age of twelve. Most days he sucks on sugarcane for breakfast and lunch. Dinner is a meal of rice and beans. He is not a legal resident of the country. Because of this, he is afraid to complain about his living conditions.

"I know something is wrong here," he told reporters. "But if we complain, the owners will call immigration on us and then where will we be?"[14]

Lebanese farm children were studied in 2000. They described their work as hard and boring. Children as young as three worked on tobacco farms with their parents. Younger children dried leaves. Older children transplanted seedlings, watered crops, weeded rows of plants, and bound leaves into bundles. They worked up to thirteen hours a day during the spring and summer seasons. Many children ended their education after elementary school.[15] Farm children in other countries work under similar conditions.

Chocolate Starts Here

It's our favorite flavor. We love it in milk, ice cream, and best of all in candy. Chocolate has more adoring fans than any movie star or basketball idol you can name. However, most of us would eat far less chocolate if we had to harvest it.

Chocolate comes from cocoa seeds that grow inside a large, leathery pod. Most cocoa plantations are in West Africa, where cocoa trees thrive in the hot, wet climates of Cameroon, Ivory Coast, Ghana, and Nigeria.

Harvesting cocoa is hard work. A child labor study in 2004 described the process. First, workers use short, curved knives on long poles to cut the pods from the trees. Then pods are gathered into baskets. The next step is to cut the pods open. Workers drag the baskets to an open area and whack open the shells using machetes. Inside are slimy seeds coated with pulp. Workers scoop out the seeds and cover them with banana leaves. The pulp is left to ferment. In nine days, when the seeds turn brown, workers spread them out on drying racks in full sunlight. The final step is to load the harvest into sacks. Growers ship the sacks to factories, where the seeds are ground into cocoa powder.[16]

Media reports in 2000 revealed widespread child labor on cocoa plantations. Industry leaders launched an investigation. Researchers found 284,000 children using machetes. Another 153,000 children sprayed crops with poisonous chemicals. Children worked twelve hours a day. Only one third of child workers attended school. Sadly, many children interviewed in the study had never tasted chocolate.[17]

Sharp Knives and Long Days

Sugar is another favorite additive for snack foods. One source of sugar is the syrup from sugarcane. Children studied in El Salvador's sugarcane fields were found working in hazardous conditions similar to those on cocoa plantations.

Children in Ivory Coast walk back from the cocoa fields, carrying fire-wood. Many children who harvest cocoa have never tasted chocolate.

Chopping down sugarcane requires strength and a sharp knife. In 2000, eleven year-old Carlos told Human Rights Watch, an activist group, about the tools he used each day. One was a sharp instrument called a *chumpa*.

"I grab the cane, cut it; grab it, cut it," said Carlos.[18] Some days he cut as much as six tons of sugarcane. He began work at 5:00 A.M. every day.

Other children in El Salvador told Human Rights Watch of blisters on their hands from acid in the sugarcane. Some young workers pointed to scars. They had hurt themselves with knives. Children spent long hours in the hot sun.[19]

An Onion on Your Hamburger

In the mid-1990s, researchers studied children on onion farms in Colombia. Four-year-olds worked alongside older children. Both children and adults were paid according to how many onions they gathered. Children gave their earnings to parents. During the harvest season, children began work as early as 4:00 A.M. and worked until 5:00 P.M. The long hours made it difficult for children to attend school.[20]

"There's a chance that when you have fried onions on your hamburger or . . . slice an onion for your evening salad, that a child has been involved in the harvest," filmmaker Len Morris told *Nightline* in 2005.[21] Morris and his partner filmed child labor in many parts of the world, including the onion fields of Batesville, Texas. Morris found children picking onions for a penny per pound.

Migrant farm worker children in America face some of the same hazards as children in other parts of the world. They can suffer from exposure to the sun, pesticides, and long hours that interfere with school. Nearly eight hundred thousand migrant farm worker children work in American fields, according to the United Farm Workers union.[22] Most live in Arizona, Texas, Florida, or on the West Coast. Children of migrant farm workers are less protected than other children in America, say reform groups.

The U.S. Labor Department explains that because the United States began as "a nation of farmers" agricultural jobs have fewer restrictions than other types of labor. A report on youth and labor published in 2000 says: "Growing up on the family farm, learning the value of hard work in the fresh air, is still viewed by many as the perfect childhood."[23]

Senator Tom Harkin of Iowa opposes the "loopholes" in American laws that allow children in agriculture to work at hazardous jobs.

> A child 10 years old can't work at McDonald's. A child under 18 in America cannot work in hazardous occupations. But in agriculture, they're working out in the hot sun picking peppers or tomatoes, subject to insecticides and pesticides and everything else. . . . And that is legal in America today.[24]

When Fishing Isn't Fun

Work in agriculture includes hunting and fishing. Most of us think of fishing as fun. We may enjoy paddling a boat or waiting for fish to nibble on our bait. However, fishing for a living can be hazardous.

Hamisi (not his real name) is an orphan in Tanzania who lives with his uncle, a fisherman. Hamisi does not attend school. Instead, he helps his uncle drag the day's catch ashore. They cut open the fish and pack the fillets with salt. Hamisi receives food and a place to live in exchange for his work. A research report on child labor in Tanzania describes his life:

> Hamisi spends many hours under the scorching sun and complains of frequent headaches. He has cut himself on several occasions with a sharp knife he uses for bisecting fish. Last year, one of his cuts became seriously infected. Several of his friends have drowned.[25]

Researchers say Hamisi is a typical child working in Tanzania's informal economy. Labor laws do not protect him, because he works for a family member. Such children may go unnoticed by local officials.

Another study in El Salvador found comparable dangers for children who fish for a living. The children waded barefoot through swamps to find mollusks buried beneath the mud. The report noted that swamp waters hold microorganisms that can cause infections. Mosquitoes and snakes that live in or around the waters pose health problems, too.[26]

Mining for Three Buckets A Day

Some mining operations are part of the informal economy. About one million children between the ages of five and seventeen work in small mines or rock quarries, according to the ILO.[27] Mining is extremely dangerous for children. They haul buckets of mud, break up rocks, sieve for ore, and climb into dark, narrow passageways. Some do it to help their families survive.

If you worked at an open-pit mine in the Democratic Republic of the Congo, you would receive an unusual form of

A fourteen-year-old Congolese boy carries a sack of rocks and dirt out of a diamond mine. About a million children worldwide work in small mines.

payment. Three buckets of mine muck—that's what children interviewed in 2005 earned for a day's work. Muck is mud. Mud may contain gold nuggets—or it may not.[28]

To get their daily share of muck, miners as young as twelve scrambled up and down the steep slopes digging for rocks that contained the precious metal. Others stood in pools of muddy water to sieve for gold ore.[29]

A twelve-year-old miner interviewed for the story said that he was an orphan. The boy had lost both parents in a regional war. The war lasted from 1998 to 2003 and destroyed the lives of four million people, including the boy's family. Now he struggled to support himself. One in four workers at the mine were between twelve and fourteen years old.[30]

Home-Based Jobs Are Growing

Home-based manufacturing is another example of work that takes place in the informal economy. The term refers to families who make a product in their homes. Children and their parents may peel prawns in Pakistan, dry tobacco leaves in Lebanon, or paint pottery in Indonesia.

Experts believe home-based work may be increasing in South Asia. They think that world attention on child labor may have frightened factory and workshop owners.[31] By sending the work to private homes, business owners can still use cheap labor. Child labor laws in India and Pakistan do not forbid this type of work.

A study conducted in 2001 found Thai children harvesting seeds in home workshops. In Indonesia, children gathered in small groups to paint designs on pottery. Girls in India sewed elaborate designs on clothing. In India and Pakistan, families also made incense sticks at home by mixing sawdust with colorful, toxic chemicals. Children formed a paste with their bare hands. They rolled the paste into sticks.[32]

Rolling Bidis in Andhra Pradesh

Bidis are small, brown cigarettes made of hand-cut tobacco. The cigarettes are wrapped in tendu leaves—a type of plant—instead of in paper. Bidi production is widespread in the south of India in states such as Andhra Pradesh. While Andhra Pradesh has several large cities, most people live in villages or on farms. Few villagers can read or write. To make ends meet, many families make bidi cigarettes in their homes for tobacco factories. Researchers believe this practice may be declining. However, it is still widespread.[33]

Dr. Rekha Pande, a researcher at the University of Hyderabad in India, conducted a study in 1995 of villagers who made bidis at home.[34] Dr. Pande found that girls and their mothers were the main laborers. Girls as young as five years old helped their mothers pack, roll, and tie off the cigarettes. Workers toiled for hours in the same position, breathing tobacco dust.[35]

Her study revealed the work to be tedious. The tobacco leaves had to be cut to the right size. To make a single bidi, the worker had to unfold a tendu leaf, measure out less than a gram of tobacco, roll up the leaf, fold the edges, and tie the end with string. Bidis were then bundled and labeled.[36]

Several health concerns emerged from the study. Workers complained of skin problems, burning eyes, and pain in their joints and limbs. Breathing tobacco dust was linked to lung diseases such as bronchitis.[37]

Bidi production does not pay well, nor is it available year round. Some families took out high-interest loans to cover expenses during off seasons, according to the study. When parents were unable to pay back the loans, they offered the services of their children in exchange.

Why Children Work

Why are so many children trapped in child labor throughout the world? The answers vary from region to region, but some factors are common. Many experts say that poverty is one of the main reasons that children work. One African boy's story illustrates the misery of poverty and shows how disease can be a contributing factor in some regions. He was only eight when his parents died from HIV/AIDS. This boy in Uganda almost dropped out of school. A relief organization called TASO (short for The AIDS Service Organization) helped him pay his tuition and other school fees. Unfortunately, no one could stop the heartache.

"I was known as 'The Son of AIDS,'" the child told Human Rights Watch in 2004. "When we were sharing desks, the kids wouldn't want to sit next to me." He recalls with sadness that even the teachers called him "the TASO child."[1]

The HIV/AIDS epidemic has killed millions of parents, leaving children homeless or in dire financial straits. Children also die from the infection. One of the hardest hit regions is sub-Saharan Africa. About 2.5 million AIDS orphans lived in Ethiopia, Mozambique, Rwanda, and Zambia in 2004. By some estimates, the number will climb to 3.8 million by 2010.[2]

Africa is not the only region at risk. India has four million people living with the disease. Other countries in Asia, Central and Eastern Europe, Latin America and elsewhere have large numbers of children and parents who have been infected.

"Every minute of every day, a child dies because of AIDS," says UNICEF's executive director Ann Veneman. The disease affects children's lives in many ways. Some die. Others are left behind to fend for themselves. Veneman observes:

> They are missing parents, missing teachers, missing treatment and care, missing protection, missing many things, except for the devastating effects of this disease."[3]

When HIV/AIDS kills one or both parents, children go to work to survive. Although public school is free in most countries, books, equipment, and uniforms are not. One report showed that few AIDS orphans can find money to go to school, let alone the time to study, particularly if they have younger brothers and sisters to feed and protect.[4]

Orphans may become involved in the worst forms of child labor, including domestic service or prostitution, according to the U.S. Department of Labor. Many children will work excessive hours for very little pay in hazardous work environments. In addition to the pain of losing their parents, AIDS orphans face hunger. They lack health care.[5]

Wars create orphans, too. In recent decades, armed conflicts have destroyed families in Africa, Asia, the Middle East, and Latin America. However, orphans are not the only children who work. Child labor has multiple causes.

Poverty, Poor Schools, Old Attitudes

UNICEF points to three conditions that contribute to child labor throughout the world: poverty, obstacles to education, and traditional attitudes.

About 600 million children in developing countries survive on less than one U.S. dollar per day.[6] When families are struggling, the money earned by a child can mean the difference between surviving or not. Roughly half of all working children also attend school, according to the ILO. Sometimes they earn money to pay for school uniforms, fees, and books. Their work makes it possible for them to stay in school.

However, poverty also drives families to choose full-time work instead of school for their children. Many countries do not offer affordable education to those who need it most. The Population Council notes that 37 million African children will not complete primary schooling. Worldwide, more than 100 million children do not go to school at all.[7] Schools in developing countries may be poorly staffed, underfunded, and costly. Even public schools often require fees for books and equipment.

For instance, in Cambodia, children from villages and farms often quit school to work in the fields. Some never go to school at all, according to a report by the U.S. State Department. Although most children complete elementary school, only 21 percent of eligible students attend secondary school. One out of two schools lack drinking water and bathrooms. Classrooms are overflowing. Books, desks, and supplies are scarce. Teachers sometimes expect private payments from families to supplement their meager salaries. This practice limits opportunities for children of the poor.[8]

Long-held social attitudes also contribute to child labor.

Attitudes are complex and range from the idea that "girls do not need school" to the belief that old ways of doing things should continue. Girls face discrimination in addition

to poverty in many African, Asian, and Middle Eastern countries. UNICEF says that out of 115 million children not enrolled in primary school, 61.5 million of them are girls.[9]

Attitudes Change Slowly

"When my children were three, I told them they must be prepared to work for the good of the family," a Pakistani mother told journalist Jonathan Silvers. She bonded her five children to masters in other towns. This mother's words suggest that she accepted child labor as a normal part of life. "I told them again and again that they would be bonded at five. And when the time came for them to go, they were prepared and went without complaint."[10]

ILO studies reveal that parents' attitudes are sometimes the result of generations of poverty. As children grow up, they repeat the actions of their parents and grandparents. Often education is not considered important.[11]

Social attitudes also influence child labor practices. For instance, India has outlawed bonded labor, but the practice still exists, particularly among some ethnic groups. Certain castes, or groups within Indian society, are considered inferior. For centuries they have received harsh treatment. Children from these disadvantaged groups make up a significant portion of child laborers, according to Human Rights Watch.[12]

Some Believe Work Is a Good Alternative

Some cultures view work as a positive learning experience. Sociology professor Loretta Bass points out that in many parts

Boys in Rangoon carry bricks at a construction site. Many poor parents expect their children to work to contribute to the family's survival.

of Africa, schooling is not always available or of a high quality. Therefore, some parents believe work offers children a better life. Many jobs are considered training. Work on the farm is a way to gain valuable survival skills. Becoming an apprentice to a skilled tailor, shoemaker, or other tradesman, many parents believe, is more practical than school.[13]

Another researcher, Manfred Liebel, interviewed a number of children in Latin America during the 1990s who wanted to work. "Either they wish to help their families or they believe it to be the only way to afford to attend school or to purchase urgently needed medicines," he writes.[14]

Corruption, Lax Laws, Mismanagement

Most people agree that child labor laws do not work when officials are corrupt. Suppose a policeman or local politician accepts a bribe from an employer. The official will then pretend not to see trafficking, sexual exploitation, or sweatshop conditions.

Dishonest political leaders have added to Africa's poverty, says professor Loretta Bass. Poverty, in turn, encourages child labor. She explains that wealthier nations have lent money to Africa in recent decades. Officials have sometimes stolen funds intended for schools, new businesses, and roads.[15] However, the people must pay back the loans. As a result, they are poorer than before.

In Africa, child labor laws are in place to keep children safe and in school. Many laws are enforced poorly, if at all, says Bass. She explains the laws have no real effect on children's lives. The laws only make government officials feel better.

She writes, "Unfortunately, legislation geared at eliminating child labor is like offering a starving child a slice of imaginary cake."[16]

7   Searching for Solutions

Poverty is often mentioned as one of the root causes of child labor. Some children work so that they can help their parents meet basic necessities such as food, clothing, and a home. Orphans often have no choice but to work. However, UNICEF disagrees that poverty must be eliminated *before* child labor can be stopped. A UNICEF report states:

> We are told we must tolerate the intolerable until world poverty is ended. . . . The fact remains that when a child is engaged in hazardous labor, someone—an employer, a customer or a parent—benefits from that labor.[1]

UNICEF observes that child labor exists because someone

takes advantage of the child. Employers may be looking for cheap labor or may want workers who are easy to control. Parents may benefit from the extra income.

Many world leaders are determined to end child labor. Programs to end child labor are in place in Tanzania, Kenya, Zimbabwe, Brazil, El Salvador, Philippines, Thailand, India, Indonesia, Nepal, Pakistan, and other countries.

Nongovernmental organizations are also hard at work to improve the lives of children. RugMark is an example of what an NGO can accomplish.

RugMark saves bonded children in the carpet weaving industry in India, Nepal, and Pakistan. Founded in 1994 by activist Kailash Satyarthi, RugMark rescues children caught in illegal labor. The group helps the children to obtain training. Rehabilitation centers provide a place for rescued children to live while they learn new skills. In 2005 RugMark reported that 3,611 rescued children were in school or day care programs.[2]

RugMark helps people buy carpets without worry. The organization gives carpet manufacturers a label to use if they have not used children in their factories. The label says "child labor free." Consumers who see the label know they are not contributing to child labor with their purchase.

The RugMark label keeps children out of factories. It offers consumers proof of quality. Manufacturers who do not use child labor are protected from boycotts. A boycott is an act of protest taken by a group of people. When shoppers boycott a product, they refuse to buy it. Sales drop. Manufacturers lose money.

RugMark publishes stories about children who have been helped through their programs. One such story is about Narayan Tiwari, who worked in a carpet factory as a child. He described long work days that lasted up to fifteen hours. Children who spun wool and wove carpets received little pay for their work. Often their meager earnings were taken away by adult family members. Children were punished severely for their mistakes. Narayan described life as a child carpet weaver as "miserable." With RugMark's help he was able to leave the factory and attend school. "Because of RugMark, now I have a pen in my hand instead of working tools, knowledge in mind and confidence towards life," said Narayan.[3]

The RugMark program illustrates how cooperation between private businesses, NGOs, and citizens can end child labor. Many industries are joining the fight. Companies that grow and process chocolate announced steps in 2002 to put an end to the worst forms of child labor. Football federations on several continents have broadcast public service messages about child labor at football games. (Football is called "soccer" in the United

A Pakistani girl weaves in a rug factory. RugMark is an NGO that is working to end child labor in this industry.

States.) During the 2004 Asian tournament, the Asian Football Confederation showed film clips on stadium screens, made public announcements, and passed out T-shirts and badges.[4]

UNICEF Identifies Solutions

Cooperation is a powerful tool to end child labor. UNICEF outlined a plan in 1997 that encouraged this approach.[5] It recommended that world governments, business leaders, members of the media, and private citizens work together to improve the lives of children.

The cornerstone of UNICEF's plan to end child labor is education. It also urges the world community to provide more resources to the poor. It is not enough to remove a child from hazardous work, says UNICEF. The child's income must be replaced so that families can survive.

In recent years, the International Program on the Elimination of Child Labour (IPEC) has helped countries put a number of programs into place to break the cycle of poverty. Some rescue programs offer small stipends, or payments, to families of working children.

Another approach is *microfinance*. These programs involve providing resources to families or individuals to help them make positive changes. In some cases, banks offer small loans to women or poor families to start a business. Retail stores offer credit to poor families. Companies may help people start and operate small service businesses. For example, GrameenPhone in Bangladesh is a large cellular phone business. This company has a program to help people set up cellular phone businesses in their villages.[6]

UNICEF urges private businesses to be responsible for their own behavior. It says that business leaders should demand that smaller companies—the ones that supply raw materials or parts—obey child labor laws. For example, a candy manufacturer might buy sugar from several sources. The candy maker should not buy sugar from suppliers that use children to harvest sugarcane.

More Than Three Decades of Progress

The International Labour Organization set the stage for modern reforms in 1973 with the adoption of the Minimum Age Convention. Children could start work at the general age of fifteen, although exceptions were made for "light work" and children in developing economies. Children were required to finish compulsory education before entering the workplace.

Public concern about child labor began to grow. The United Nations declared 1979 to be the International Year of the Child. In 1989, the UN passed the Convention on the Rights of the Child (CRC). The CRC clearly states the human rights of children everywhere. No other document has been so widely ratified.

During these early years, NGOs, activists, private businesses, and concerned government officials were hard at work in many countries. They corrected abuses wherever possible. However, the global movement gathered fresh energy in 1999. That year marked the passage of ILO Convention 182. So far, 158 countries have ratified the Worst Forms of Child Labor Convention. Leaders agreed to put programs into place, monitor abuses, pass legislation, and to help one another.

Millennium Development Goals Point the Way

In 2000, world leaders gathered at the Millennium Summit to discuss the state of society. They envisioned a global community with more peace and prosperity for everyone. Leaders of 189 countries set eight goals:

1. to reduce poverty and hunger
2. to give every child a basic education
3. to provide equal treatment for girls and women
4. to improve the health of children

5. to improve the health of mothers
6. to fight deadly diseases such as HIV/AID.
7. to protect the environment
8. to cooperate to help developing countries.[7]

Government leaders set 2015 as a deadline f ducing poverty by half and for meeting the other goals.

Every one of the Millennium Development Goal (DGs) helps children, according to Ann M. Veneman, execu direc-tor of UNICEF.[8] Children's lives are at stake, but sc the futures of nations, according to UNICEF:

> Countries struggle to develop when their citizens grow up 1 nourished, poorly educated or ravaged by disease. These fact perpetuate poverty and low productivity and may lead to instabil. or even spill over into violence and armed conflict.[9]

So, UNICEF says, the millennium goals will both help c dren and reduce strife among nations.[10]

Child Labor Decreasing

The child labor reform movement appears to be on the right track. In 2004 there were 28 million fewer children in the work force than in 2000. The ILO offers several reasons for the decline. Governments have been willing to make changes. Programs to reduce poverty have been successful. More children have been able to go to school.

Some countries have been more successful than others at removing children from child labor. Only 5 percent of children in Latin America and the Caribbean were child laborers in 2004. By contrast, Africa is the region that has had the most difficult time achieving its goals for ending child labor. In 2004 the ILO reported 50 million children at work in the region.[11]

However, Africa also has some success stories to share. IPEC reports that many African governments have made education a top goal. Uganda is a good example.[12] Uganda is one of the world's est countries. Before 1997, families spent roughly one fif their income to send a child to school. Parents had to pay buy books and materials, and pay parent-teacher associ costs. As a result, few families could afford school. The rnment corrected the problem. New federal funds were d to put children between the ages of six and twelve into ool. Enrollments have nearly doubled.[13]

erts agree that education is the best way to reduce child lab Studies show that educated mothers have healthier children. Well-informed parents are less likely to keep children out of ool. An educated child will earn more money as an adult. Erts say education can break the cycle of poverty.

The U.S. Department of Labor explains the benefits to society:

A society of educated citizens benefits from individuals who are healthier, more involved in the political process, less dependent on social support programs, less inclined to a life of crime, more likely to save, and more likely to innovate.[15]

Child laborers earn about one fifth of what an adult earns.[16] By contrast, the financial reward for educating a child is great. For every dollar a country invests in a child's basic education, the government receives six dollars back (in terms of taxes and savings).[17]

How IPEC Helps Children

A former child worker in Bangladesh told her story at an international conference on child labor. Julekha attended school in Bangladesh until the age of nine. Then her father became sick. She had to drop out of school and go to work in a garment factory.

Bangladesh garment factories make shirts, blue jeans, and other items for the worldwide market. Workers in a garment factory typically sit for long hours in the same position. Sewing machines have rapidly moving needles that pose a safety hazard.

Julekha was rescued by IPEC representatives. They removed her from the factory and allowed her to go to school. They gave

Ishmael Beah, a former child soldier in Sierra Leone, speaks at a conference sponsored by UNICEF. This agency of the United Nations fights to end child labor.

Julekha's family a stipend to make up for her wages. Now she wants to be a teacher.[18]

IPEC programs operate in many countries. Programs in Asia remove children from footwear factories in Indonesia and from armed conflict in the Philippines and Sri Lanka. IPEC targets bonded labor in Nepal and carpet weaving in Pakistan.

In Africa, IPEC helps government leaders remove children from armed conflict in Burundi, the Democratic Republic of the Congo, and Rwanda. Efforts to stop child trafficking focus on nine countries, including Benin, Togo, and Ghana. In West and Central Africa, children are removed from cocoa plantations. Programs in Uganda and Zambia help girls caught in domestic service.[19]

In Latin America, IPEC promotes public awareness campaigns. Programs encourage families to remove children from making fireworks in El Salvador and Guatemala and from mining in Nicaragua, Ecuador, Bolivia, and Peru. Many countries now provide skills training for young people. Overall, IPEC has helped more than a million children worldwide.[20]

NGOs That Work With IPEC

A government journal published the story of a man named Christopher Wakiraza who found a way to help street children. Wakiraza was a young college graduate when he founded Kids in Need (KIN). Today KIN works as a partner with IPEC. Kids receive education, counseling, and health care. KIN encourages children to paint colorful city murals along public walkways. The murals allow children to express their feelings. They also help townspeople understand the problems of homeless children.

Wakiraza told the story of how his organization started. Soon after he graduated from college, while walking one day in Kampala City in Uganda, Wakiraza saw street children throwing rocks at a car. He followed the two boys to a park and asked their names.

He learned that one child sold pineapples for a living while the other boy worked at a shoeshine stall. Finding enough food to eat was a daily struggle for the boys. Wakiraza kept checking on the children. When one of them landed in jail, Wakiraza decided to get involved. He rented a house with the help of local priests. Ten street children carried their cardboard boxes and plastic bags—what they used for mattresses and blankets—into the shelter. "And thus was born Kids in Need," says Wakiraza.[21]

Organizations such as KIN help families and communities. NGOs do important work. However, they cannot make lasting reforms without a strong commitment from their national leaders. The ILO says national governments have to take child labor seriously for a country to make progress.

Success in Brazil

Brazil has been successful in reducing child labor. The number of working children has dropped by 50 percent in recent years.[22] Government leaders are largely credited for the improvement.

IPEC reports that when President Fernando Henrique Cardoso took office in 1995, he was determined to end child labor. He started a program called the Bolsa-Escola. Poor families received stipends so that children could stay in school. His successor, Luis Inácio Lula da Silva, continued the payments.

Private businesses and citizens also took steps to end child labor. Business groups established a labeling system for customers. Shoppers who bought toys in Brazil could look for the "child labor free" stamp. Similar labels were available for automobiles, shoes, sugar, and other products.

Business leaders took responsibility in other ways. For example, shoe factories in the town of Franco discovered that children were working for smaller companies that supplied parts to the shoe industry. The factory owners developed a project to put boys and girls back in school. The factories also sponsored after-school programs so that former working children could enjoy music, sports, and cultural events.[23]

India's Progress Slower

In contrast to Brazil's dramatic progress, India is moving more slowly towards ending its child labor problems. Despite many laws, India has more child laborers than any other nation. In fact, because of its rapid growth in population, India's child labor pool *grew* between 1991 and 2001 by one million boys and girls.[24]

The problem is not a lack of child labor laws. The Indian Constitution protects children younger than fourteen from hazardous jobs, particularly in factories and mines. It calls for safe working conditions, rest periods, and free schooling for children. During the last fifty years, India has ratified six international child labor conventions, but it has never enforced them.

A law passed in 1987 created National Child Labor Projects. The projects save children from dead-end jobs and dangerous work. Rescued children receive training, medicine, and healthy food. India has 150 child rescue programs operating in thirteen states.

However, experts say that for every child saved, countless more are still at work. One method for estimating child labor is to compare the number of school-aged children to the number of enrollments. If children are not in school, say researchers, they might be at work. India's education department says 25 million children between the ages of six to fourteen are not attending school. Nongovernmental groups say the number is much higher—65 million![25]

Nine in ten children work in rural areas. For example, reports say that cottonseed growers in Andhra Pradesh may use children in the fields, particularly girls. In urban areas children work in private homes, hotels, and restaurants. A smaller number of children reportedly work in manufacturing; weave carpets; spin silk and cotton; make electric light bulbs and bangles; sew sports balls and leather goods; cut diamonds; and make padlocks.[26]

A study of child labor in the 1990s revealed the hazards of lock manufacturing. Making locks involves three dangerous activities: polishing, electroplating, and spray painting, said the report. Children who polish metal can inhale metal dust or be injured by the buffing machine. Spray-painting equipment emits harmful fumes. Electroplating uses toxic chemicals. Children who stick metal parts into vats of chemicals can receive burns. They also risk electric shocks.[27]

India's children also work in brick kilns and quarries.

A nine-year-old girl carries a heavy basket of topsoil at a mine near Delhi. India's progress to end dangerous child labor has been slow.

Documentary filmmakers found girls working in gravel quarries. The filmmakers reported that girls held pots of gravel half their weight on their heads. Rock dust filled the air at the worksite. The girls wore no protective breathing masks.[28]

India's labor ministry says "extreme poverty" is the primary cause of child labor in the country. Jobs are scarce for many people. Work also varies from season to season for people who live in rural areas. Parents and children often work together to survive.[29]

More Commitment Needed

India's children are not alone. Despite international laws and public support, millions of children continue to work in hazardous conditions throughout the world. Activists worry in particular about children who work in the informal economy, out of sight of labor inspectors and the general public.

"These are the children most in need: the poorest, the most vulnerable, the exploited and the abused," said Ann M. Veneman in a 2006 address.[30] She said more commitment is needed to reach every child:

> Reaching these children—many of whom are currently beyond the reach of laws, programs, research and budgets—is a challenge. And yet, meeting our commitments to children will be possible only if we approach the challenge head-on.[31]

The ILO identified both progress and challenges in its second global report on child labor released in 2006. UN agencies, world governments, NGOs, private businesses and citizens were urged to continue their efforts to reduce child labor. The report acknowledged that children have an important role to play. Working children can provide information about their situation, offer opinions, take part in debates, make their views known to lawmakers, and make a difference in their communities, suggests the ILO.[32] Many people recognize that some of the strongest voices for reform come from kids.

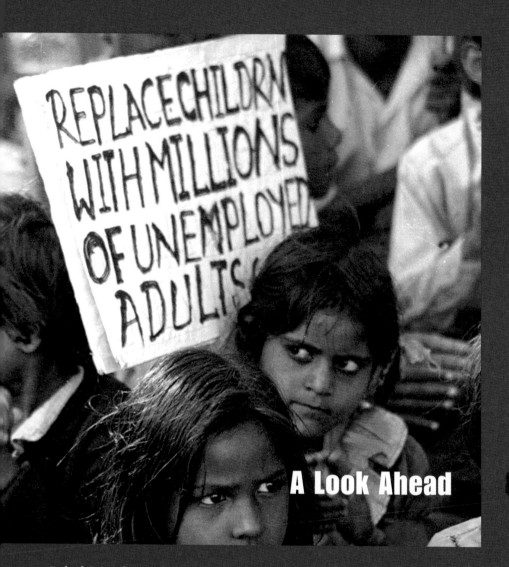

A Look Ahead

Iqbal Masih made people care about child labor. In his short life he won honors from the International Labour Organization for his courage in speaking out to the public. Reebok's Human Rights Foundation awarded him their Youth in Action Award. ABC News featured him as a Person of the Week.[1] He brought attention to the suffering of children. He helped thousands of Pakistani children escape from bonded labor in brick and textile factories and other industries.

Iqbal was born in Pakistan near the city of Lahore. At the age of four, he was sold to a carpet loom owner. His parents needed money for the wedding of his older brother. For six years Iqbal was chained to his work station. At times he was beaten.[2]

He never grew very tall, but he had powerful ideas. He escaped from his master and joined the Bonded Labor Liberation Front (BLLF) of Pakistan. As he spoke out about the evils of child labor, he gained world attention and perhaps some enemies, too.

Iqbal was shot and killed in April 1995.[3] He was thirteen years old. The BLLF blamed local carpet manufacturers for the murder. According to the organization, the carpet manufacturers were angry because Iqbal had made them look bad to the public.[4] The charges were never proved.

Even after his death, Iqbal continued to inspire people. Reebok made a grant to UNICEF in Iqbal's name. The money helps child laborers in south Asia go to school.[5] Middle school students in Quincy, Massachusetts, raised money to build a school in Pakistan in memory of Iqbal.[6]At the age of twelve, Craig Kielburger of Canada was so moved by Iqbal's murder that he started a children's foundation called "Free the Children." Today that foundation raises money to improve the lives of child laborers and their families in many countries.

Tomorrow's Leaders

Through UNICEF and other organizations, children are getting involved in the child labor reform movement. As today's children become tomorrow's elected officials and taxpayers, they have the opportunity to make greater changes.

Kielburger says, "We must create a new generation willing to help and to share with the impoverished people of the world."[7] In 2002, young delegates from many countries gathered in New York for the first United Nations Special Session on Children. Child delegates came to tell leaders about the needs of children. They met for three days in a Children's Forum. They talked about abuse in the workplace. They also shared ideas on education and improving healthcare. At the end of three days, they wrote down their ideas to present to world leaders. The statement included their views on poverty, education, health, and other children's issues.[8]

Two young people were selected to present the statement to the UN General Assembly. Gabriela, a thirteen-year-old delegate from Bolivia, was one of the children. "We want a world fit for children," she told members of the United Nations. She said that such a world would be a good place for everyone.[9]

Children are getting involved in the child labor reform movement through UNICEF and other organizations.

At the end of the United Nations Special Session on Children, member nations adopted a new resolution. They put their ideas in a document called "A World Fit for Children." They promised to "put children first." They outlined twenty-one goals to help children have healthier, happier lives. They promised to lead the global movement for children and make lasting changes.[10]

Child laborers themselves are taking part in the child labor reform movement. Groups of working children in Africa, India, and Latin America have organized to make improvements in their situations. In 1991 a group of working children formed the Bal Mazdoor Sangh (Child Worker's Union) in Delhi with the help of a local NGO called Butterflies. Author Anthony Swift studied the group, many of whom were street children. They also worked in cafes, garages, and various small businesses.[11] Butterflies, the NGO, encouraged the children to tackle issues that were important to them. For example, the children wanted education and health information. Butterflies supplied street educators who provided training in hygiene and common diseases. Teachers also set up classes in a variety of settings, even on the streets. The children also setup a credit union for their members, which gave them a way to borrow money for small projects. Swift writes that the children wanted to see an end to the worst forms of child labor, but did not want all children's work to be banned. They felt this would only create more suffering.[12]

The National Movement of Working Children (NMWC) in India formed in 1999. The NMWC is a national federation of working children's organizations. It is made up of more than fourteen thousand children from four states who help each other solve problems. The children offer protection and information to one another. In one organization, children pooled their money and opened a bank account. This was important, since children often had no safe place to keep their earnings. Members of another group banded together to protect a girl who was being threatened by neighborhood bullies. In 2003, the NMWC wrote a report to the international Committee on the Rights of the Child asking world leaders to hear firsthand about the problems facing working children.[13]

Author Manfred Liebel, a professor of sociology at the Technical University of Berlin, reports that working children in seventeen towns of West Africa began organizing in the early 1990s to provide mutual support and protection. They organized with the help of Enda Jeunesse Action, an NGO based in Dakar, Senegal. For example, one local group helped its members buy shoeshine products at a reduced rate. They also organized medical care and language lessons. The children identified four basic rights for themselves: "the right to health; the right to security; the right to education; and the right to remain in the villages."[14] Children met in their own communities to solve problems. They also traveled to national and international conferences to share information and ideas.[15]

Goals may vary somewhat from country to country and from one organization to the next, but a single theme characterizes these groups: working children want to have a say in shaping their futures.

Craig Kielburger, shown in 1996 at age thirteen, founded Free the Children in response to the murder of Iqbal Masih, a bonded laborer who fought back.

You Can Help

There are many ways to get involved. Even small efforts count. Kielburger tells of an eight-year-old boy in Canada who raised $31.27 for Free the Children by collecting empty soda bottles at his trailer camp.[16]

Some basic ideas to get you started are as follows:

- Learn more about the issue. Visit educational Web sites or your public library. The more you know, the more you can encourage others to get involved.

- Visit UNICEF'S Web site for young people. Here kids share ideas and information. Survivors of child labor tell their stories.

- Contact the Child Labor Coalition (CLC) in Washington, D.C. to find more organizations fighting child labor. The CLC is the largest association of child labor organizations in the United States. You can write to them at:1701 K Street, NW, Suite 1200, Washington, DC 20006.

- The Global Campaign for Education maintains a Web site for students. You can take part in activities that help send children to school in other countries. Activities include making a poster to tell classmates about the 100 million children who are not attending school.

- Migrant farm worker children in America often work in conditions similar to those in developing countries. Contact the Association of Farmworker Opportunity Programs (AFOP) for more information. Send letters to: 1726 M Street NW, Suite 800, Washington, D.C. 20036.

- Documentary filmmaker Len Morris suggests buying organic fruits and vegetables.[17] Organic farmers do not use pesticides. Poisonous chemicals are one of the worst hazards for children who work in agriculture.

Your Voice Counts

Child labor is not new. Industrialized nations once employed large numbers of children in mines, factories, brick kilns, and other businesses. Author Hugh Cunningham concludes that four basic factors explain the decline of child labor in western societies. Society gradually changed as family incomes rose, technology in factories lessened the need for cheap labor, legislation urged families to make different choices, and new ideas took root about the rights of children.[18]

The current child labor reform movement aims to achieve some of the same goals. Reformers want to see poverty eliminated so that families can afford to put children in schools. They also urge more respect for the rights of children.

Reformers in all walks of life are making a difference and every effort helps. Children are an important part of the solution. Your voice counts. Many children—like the Canadian boy who collected empty soda bottles to raise money—show what a single determined person can do.

Chapter Notes

Chapter 1 Bleak Futures, Bright Hopes

1. "Trafficking and Forced Labor of Children in the Gulf Region," Anti-Slavery International, Submission to United Nations Commission on Human Rights, June 2005, <http://www.antislavery.org/archive/submission2005-cameljockeys.htm> (January 25, 2006).

2. Ibid.

3. "7,000 Pakistani 'camel kids' stranded in Gulf," *The Peninsula Online: Qatar's Leading English Daily*, July 19, 2005, <http://www.thepeninsulaquatar.com> (January 25, 2006).

4. "The Facts About Children Trafficked for Use as Camel Jockeys," U.S. Department of State, August 8, 2005, <http://www.state.gov/g/tip/rls.fs.2005/50940.htm> (August 23, 2005).

5. Ibid.

6. Ibid.

7. "50 more rescued underage jockeys from UAE will arrive back home next week," Ansar Burney Welfare Trust, July 2, 2005, <http://www.ansarburney.com/news27.htm> (August 23, 2005).

8. Ibid.

9. Danna Harman, "Rein of the Robo-Jockey," *The Christian Science Monitor*, February 20, 2007, p. 20.

10. Ibid.

11. Catherine Chen, telephone interview, July 26, 2006.

12. *Trafficking in Persons Report*, U.S. Department of State, Office to Monitor and Combat Trafficking in Persons, June 3, 2005, p. 10, <http://www.state.gov/g/tip/rls/tiprpt/2005/46903.htm> (August 31, 2005).

13. "The End of Child Labour: Within Reach," International Labour Organization, May 2006, p. 23, <http://www.ilo.org/dyn/declaris/DECLARATIONWEB.INDEXPAGE/> (February 25, 2007).

14. Ibid., p. 6.

15. "New ILO Report shows marked decline in child labour

worldwide, Believes its worst forms can be eliminated in 10 years," International Labour Organization, press release, May 2006, <http://www.ilo.org/public/english/bureau/inf/pr/2006/15.htm> (February 25, 2007).

16. "Fact Sheet—Global: Facts on Child Labour," International Labour Organization, June 2005, <http://www.ilo.org/dyn/declaris/ DECLARATIONWEB.INDEXPAGE> (February 25, 2007).

17. *Every Child Counts: New Global Estimates on Child Labor* (Geneva: International Labour Organization, International Program on the Elimination of Child Labor, and Statistical Information and Monitoring Program on Child Labor, 2002), p. 25.

18. Ibid., pp. 25, 27.

19. "Fact Sheet—Global: Facts on Child Labour."

20. "The Alternate Report," The National Movement of Working Children, India, July, 2003, <http://www.workingchild.org/ prota12.htm> (February 18, 2007).

21. "The End of Child Labour: Within Reach," p. 79.

22. Ibid., p. 9.

23. "About the ILO," International Labour Organization, n.d., <http://www.ilo.org/global/About_the_ILO/lang—en/index.htm> (May 14, 2007).

24. Ann M. Veneman, "Veneman remarks at launch of State of the World's Children 2006: Excluded and Invisible," December 14, 2005, <http://www.unicef.org/media/media_30462.html> (January 23, 2006).

25. Ibid.

Chapter 2   Children at Work

1. Ben White, "Children, Work, and Child Labor," *Development and Change*, 1994, p. 873.

2. *Report on the Youth Labor Force*, U.S. Department of Labor, 2000, p. 4, <http://www.bls.gov/opub/rylfhome.html> (January 23, 2006).

3. Ibid.

4. Ibid., p. 3

5. John Brown, "A Memoir of Robert Blincoe (1828)," *Encyclopaedia of British History: 1500–1980 Online*, n.d., <http://www.spartacus.schoolnet.co.uk/Iraccidents.htm> (February 7, 2006).

6. White, pp. 854–855.

7. Robert G. McIntosh, *Boys in the Pits: Child Labor in Coal Mining* (Montreal: McGill-Queen's, 2000), p. 4.

8. Ibid., p. 8.

9. Ibid., p. 3.

10. Ibid.

11. Ibid.

12. Ibid.

13. "Child Labor Reform Exhibits," Wirtz Labor Library, U.S. Department of Labor, n.d., <http://www.dol.gov/oasam/library/special/childlabor_4.htm> (January 12, 2006).

14. Ibid.

15. Henry P. Guzda, "Danger: Children at Work—A Bibliographic Time Capsule," U.S. Department of Labor, January 1998, <http://www.dol.gov/oasam/library/special/child/childexh.htm> (January 12, 2006).

16. Ibid.

Chapter 3 Abuses in the Workplace

1. Jonathan Silvers, "Child Labor in Pakistan," *The Atlantic Monthly*, February 1996, p. 83.

2. Ibid.

3. Ibid.

4. *Every Child Counts: New Global Estimates on Child Labor* (Geneva: International Labour Organization, International Program on the Elimination of Child Labor, and Statistical Information and Monitoring Program on Child Labor, 2002), p. 32.

5. Ibid., pp. 32, 33.

6. "C182 Worst Forms of Child Labour Convention, 1999,"

International Labour Organization, 2006, <http://www.ilo.org/ilolex/cgi-lex/convde.pl?C182> (March 27, 2007).

7. "Convention on the Rights of the Child," UNICEF, n.d., <http://www.unicef.org/crc/fulltext.htm> (October 15, 2005).

8. *The State of the World's Children, 1997 Report*, UNICEF, 1997, p. 32, <http://www.unicef.org/sowc97> (January 6, 2006).

9. Correspondence with Geoffrey Keele, UNICEF, May 16, 2007; "Children Out of Sight, Out of Mind, Out of Reach," UNICEF press release, December 14, 2006.

10. Based on a phone interview with Micheline Slattery, August 2006.

11. "The relationship between child domestic servitude and the sexual exploitation of children," Anti-Slavery International, 2002, <http://www.antislavery.org/archive/submission/submission2002-childlabor.htm> (February 14, 2006).

12. Ibid.

13. Omolara Dakore Oyalde, "Child Domestic Labor in Lusaka, A Gender Perspective: The Case of Kamwala, Kabwata, Libala, Chilenje, Woodlands Extension, Nyumba-Yana," UNICEF, September 2000, p. 5, <http://www.unicef.org/evaldatabase/files/ZAM_00-004.pdf> (November 16, 2005).

14. Ibid., p. 68.

15. *Every Child Counts: New Global Estimates on Child Labor*, p. 25.

16. *The State of the World's Children, 1997 Report*, p. 35.

17. Shiva Sharma, Bijendra Basnyat, and Ganesh G.C., "Nepal, Bonded Labour Among Child Workers of the Kamaiya System: A Rapid Assessment," International Labour Organization, November 2001, pp. 7, 10, <www.ilo.org/public/english/standards/ipec/simpoc/nepal/ra/bonded.pdf> (March 3, 2007).

18. Nelien Haspels and Michele Jankanish, eds., *Action Against Child Labor* (Geneva: International Labour Office, 2000), p. 188.

19. *Trafficking in Persons Report*, U.S. Department of State, Office to Monitor and Combat Trafficking in Persons, June 3, 2005, p. 22, <http://www.state.gov/g/tip/rls/tiprpt/2005/46903.htm> (August 31, 2005).

20. *Every Child Counts: New Global Estimates on Child Labour*, p. 27.

21. "Facts on Agriculture," International Labour Organization, n.d., <http://www.ilo.org/public/english/bureau/inf/download/wssd/pdf/agriculture.pdf> (March 3, 2007).

22. Martin J. Levine, *Children for Hire: The Perils of Child Labor in the United States* (Westport, Conn.: Praeger, 2003), p. 42.

23. Based on a phone interview with Eulogio Alejandre, July 2006.

24. *Cambodia: Country Report on Human Rights Practices for 2004*, Section 5, Children, U.S. Department of State, February 28, 2005, <http://www.state.gov/g/drl/rls/hrrpt/2004/41638.htm> (October 15, 2005).

25. *The State of the World's Children, 1997 Report*, p. 43.

26. Loretta E. Bass, *Child Labor in Sub-Saharan Africa* (Boulder, Colo.: Lynne Rienner, 2004), pp. 83–84.

27. Ibid., p. 83.

28. Henrietta Abane, "'The girls do not learn hard enough so they cannot do certain types of work': Experiences from an NGO sponsored gender sensitization workshop in a Southern Ghanaian community," *Community Development Journal*, vol. 39, no. 1, 2004, pp. 49–61.

29. *The State of the World's Children, 1997 Report*, p. 44.

30. Douglas L. Kruse and Douglas Mahoney. "Illegal Child Labor In the United States: Prevalence And Characteristics," *International Labour Relations Review*, vol. 54, no. 1, October 2000, pp. 17–40.

31. "Commercial Child Sexual Exploitation: 'The Most Hidden Form of Child Abuse,' says Penn Professor," University of Pennsylvania, press release, September 10, 2001.

32. Ibid.

33. Amy O'Neill Richard, *International Trafficking in Women to the United States: A Contemporary Manifestation of Slavery and Organized Crime* (Washington, D.C.: U.S. State Department, 2000), p. iii.

Chapter 4 Trapped in Slave Labor

1. "ILO releases new study on forced labour," ILO press release, May 11, 2005.

2. "Burundi Rebels Abduct Students to Fight in War," *Washington Post*, November 10, 2001, <http://www.washingtonpost.com/wp-dyn/articles/A5320-2001Nov9.html> (January 22, 2006).

3. Ibid.

4. Loretta E. Bass, *Child Labor in Sub-Saharan Africa* (Boulder, Colo.: Lynne Rienner, 2004), p. 36.

5. "Conversations with Former Child Soldiers," *Children in the Crossfire—Event Overview*, U.S. Department of Labor, Bureau of International Labor Affairs, May 7–8, 2003, pp. 32–33, <http://www.dol.gov/ilab/programs/iclp/childsoldiers/event_overview.htm> (January 12, 2006).

6. Ibid., p. 32.

7. Ibid., p. 13.

8. "Some Facts," Coalition to Stop the Use of Child Soldiers, 2006, <http://www.child-soldiers.org/childsoldiers/some-facts> (January 26, 2006).

9. Rodrique Ngowi, "Lost Generation Hurts Uganda," *The Advocate*, December 24, 2005, p. 13A.

10. Ibid.

11. Ibid.

12. "Conversations with Former Child Soldiers," p. 13.

13. Ibid., p. 6.

14. Ibid., p. 4.

15. *Adult Wars, Child Soldiers,* UNICEF, 2002, p. 25, <http://www.unicef.org/publications/index_4269.html> (January 23, 2006).

16. Ibid.

17. Ibid., pp. 8, 73.

18. "Conversations with Former Child Soldiers," p. 30.

19. *Trafficking in Persons Report*, U.S. Department of State, Office to Monitor and Combat Trafficking in Persons, June 3, 2005, p. 10,

<http://www.state.gov/g/tip/rls/tiprpt/2005/46903.htm>
(August 31, 2005).

20. *Every Child Counts: New Global Estimates on Child Labor* (Geneva: International Labour Organization, International Program on the Elimination of Child Labor, and Statistical Information and Monitoring Program on Child Labor, 2002), p. 25.

21. *Thailand: Country Report on Human Rights Practices for 2004*, Section 5, U.S. Department of State, February 28, 2005, <http://www.state.gov/g/drl/rls/hrrpt/2004/41661.htm> (October 15, 2005).

22. *Synopsis of Report on the Trafficking of Children Between Benin and Gabon*, Section 2, Anti-Slavery International, 1999, <http://www.antislavery.org/archive/other/trafficking-benin-synopsis.htm> (October 9, 2005).

23. *The State of the World's Children, 2006 Report* (New York: UNICEF, 2006), p. 50.

24. *Trafficking in Persons Report*, p. 16.

25. Ibid.

26. Ibid., p. 9.

27. *Every Child Counts: New Global Estimates on Child Labor*, p. 27.

28. *Thailand: Country Report on Human Rights Practices for 2004*, pp. 20–21.

29. *Trafficking in Persons Report*, p. 22.

30. Nelien Haspels and Michele Jankanish, eds., *Action Against Child Labor* (Geneva: International Labour Office, 2000), p. 191.

31. Ibid.

Chapter 5 At Work in the Informal Economy

1. "Fact Sheet—Global: Facts on Child Labour," International Labour Organization, <http://www.ilo.org/dyn/declaris/DECLARATIONWEB.INDEXPAGE> (February 25, 2007).

2. Ibid.

3. Ibid.

4. Loretta E. Bass, *Child Labor in Sub-Saharan Africa* (Boulder, Colo.: Lynne Rienner, 2004), p. 5.

5. Nicole Hill, "Lives Recycled in Argentina," *The Christian Science Monitor,* January 25, 2006, p. 20.

6. *Understanding Children's Work in El Salvador* (San Jose, Costa Rica: International Labour Organization, International Program on the Elimination of Child Labor, and Statistical Information and Monitoring Program on Child Labor, 2004), p. 53.

7. C. Kadonay, M. Madihi, and S. Mtwana, *Tanzania Child Labor in the Informal Sector: A Rapid Assessment* (Geneva: International Labour Office, 2002), p. 42.

8. Anthony G. Freeman, Testimony, Hearing before the Subcommittee on International Economic Policy and Trade of the Committee on International Relations House of Representatives, 158th Congress, October 22, 1997, p. 55.

9. International Labour Organization, "Facts on Agriculture" (Geneva: International Labour Office, n.d.)., p. 1.

10. Ibid.

11. Rahel Mathews, Chen Reig, and Vincent Iacopino, "Child Labor, A Matter of Health and Human Rights," *The Journal of Ambulatory Care Management,* April-June, 2003, p. 182.

12. Ibid.

13. Ibid.

14. Danna Harman, "Haitian Cane-Cutters Struggle," *The Christian Science Monitor*, February 1, 2006, p. 14.

15. Consultation and Research Institute, *Lebanon: Child Labor on Tobacco Plantations: A Rapid Assessment* (Geneva: International Labour Office, 2002), pp. 11, viii, ix.

16. "Hazardous Child Labor in Agriculture: Cocoa," Safety and Health Fact Sheet, International Program for the Elimination of Child Labor, March 2004, <http://www.ilo.org/public/english/standards/ipec/themes/cocoa/index.htm> (March 3, 2007).

17. Ibid.

18. *El Salvador, Turning A Blind Eye, Hazardous Child Labor in El*

Salvador's Sugarcane Cultivation (New York: Human Rights Watch, 2000), p. 3.

19. Ibid., p. 11.

20. Maria Cristina Salazar and Walter Alarcon Glasinovich, eds., *Child Work and Education: Five Case Studies From Latin America* (Brookfield, Vt.: Ashgate, 1999), pp. 42, 44, 45.

21. "Stolen Childhoods," transcript, *Nightline: ABC News,* June 15, 2005, p. 6.

22. "Children in the Fields: The Inequitable Treatment of Child Farmworkers," Association of Farmworker Opportunity Programs, n.d., p. 1, <http://www.afop.org/childlabor.htm> (May 7, 2007).

23. *Report on the Youth Labor Force,* U.S. Department of Labor, 2000, p. 4, <http://www.bls.gov/opub/rylfhome.html> (January 23, 2006).

24. "Stolen Childhoods."

25. Kadonay, Madihi, and Mtwana, p. ix.

26. *Understanding Children's Work in El Salvador,* p. 52.

27. "The burden of gold: Child labour in small-scale mines and quarries," *World of Work,* January 12, 2006, <http://www.ilo.org/public/english/bureau/inf/magazine/54/mines.htm> (February 5, 2006).

28. Abraham McLaughlin, "Digging for 'Tainted Gold' in Congo," *The Christian Science Monitor,* August 25, 2005, p. 12.

29. Ibid.

30. Ibid.

31. Santosh Mehrotra and Mario Biggeri, *The Subterranean Child Labor Force: Subcontracted Home Based Manufacturing in Asia* (Florence: UNICEF, 2002), p. 2.

32. Ibid., pp. 40–42.

33. Ibid., p. 17.

34. Lakshmidhar Mishra, *Child Labor in India* (New York: Oxford University Press, 2000), p. 59.

35. Ibid., p. 63.

36. Ibid.

37. Ibid., p. 64.

Chapter 6   Why Children Work

1. "Children's testimonies from *Letting Them Fail: Government Neglect and the Right to Education for Children Affected by AIDS*," Human Rights Watch, October 10, 2005, <http://hrw.org/english/docs/2005/01/07/safric11841_txt.htm> (October 29, 2005).

2. *Combating Exploitive Child Labor Through Education in the Middle East and North Africa Region; Combating Exploitive Child Labor Through Education in Ethiopia, Mozambique, Rwanda, and Zambia*, U.S. Department of Labor, ILAB Federal Register Notice, June 3, 2004, vol. 69, no.107, p. 31421.

3. Ann M. Veneman, Remarks, "Unite For Children, Unite Against AIDS," UNICEF, press release, October 25, 2005, <http://www.unicef.org/uniteforchildren/press/press_29410.htm> (December 12, 2005).

4. "Africa: Neglect of AIDS Orphans Fuels School Drop-Out," Human Rights Watch, press release, October 11, 2005, <http://hrw.org/english/docs/2005/10/07/safric11838_txt.htm> (October 29, 2005).

5. Federal Register, p. 31431.

6. "UNICEF at a Glance," UNICEF, 2004, p. 24, <http://www.unicef.org/publications/files/UNICEF_Glance_ENG.pdf> (March 3, 2007).

7. "The Scale of the Problem," Global Campaign for Education, n.d., <http://www.campaignforeducationusa.org/facts_default.asp> (March 3, 2007).

8. *Cambodia: Country Report on Human Rights Practices for 2004*, U.S. Department of State, February 28, 2005, p. 26, <http://www.state.gov/g/drl/rls/hrrpt/2004/41638.htm> (October 15, 2005).

9. *Children out of School: Measuring Exclusion from Primary Education*, UNESCO Institute for Statistics, Montreal, 2005,

pp. 17, 19, <http://www.ibe.unesco.org/cops/Animation/UNICEF_%20UESCOrepchild.pdf> (May 22, 2007).

10. Jonathan Silvers, "Child Labor in Pakistan," *The Atlantic Monthly*, February 1996, p. 82.

11. International Labour Organization, *IPEC Action Against Child Labor: Highlights 2004* (Geneva: International Labour Office, 2004), p. 51.

12. "Small Change: Bonded Child Labor in India's Silk Industry," Human Rights Watch, January 2003, <http://www.hrw.org/reports/2003/india/India0103.htm#P169_20786> (March 3, 2007).

13. Loretta E. Bass, *Child Labor in Sub-Saharan Africa* (Boulder, Colo.: Lynne Rienner, 2004), p. 181.

14. Manfred Liebel, Bernd Overwien, and Albert Recknagel, eds., *Working Children's Protagonism: Social Movements and Empowerment in Latin America, Africa and India* (Frankfurt: IKO, 2001), p. 93.

15. Bass, p. 53.

16. Ibid., p. 62.

Chapter 7 Searching for Solutions

1. *The State of the World's Children, 1997 Report*, UNICEF, 1997, p. 20, <http://www.unicef.org/sowc97> (January 6, 2006).

2. RugMark Foundation, "Annual Report 2005," 2006, p. 6, <http://www.rugmark.org/index.php?cid=16> (March 6, 2007).

3. Ibid., p. 7.

4. *IPEC Action Against Child Labor: Highlights 2004* (Geneva: International Labour Office, 2004), p. 27.

5. "Summary, Taking Action," *The State of the World's Children, 1997 Report*, UNICEF, 1997, <http://www.unicef.org/sowc97/report> (January 6, 2006).

6. *Microfinance and the Millennium Development Goals* (New York: UNICEF, 2005), p. 16.

7. Ibid., p. 19.

8. *The State of the World's Children, 2006 Report* (New York: UNICEF, 2006), p. vii.

9. Ibid., p. 6.

10. Ibid.

11. "New ILO Report shows marked decline in child labour worldwide, Believes its worst forms can be eliminated in 10 years," International Labour Organization, press release, May 2006, <http://www.ilo.org/public/english/bureau/inf/pr/2006/15.htm> (February 25, 2007).

12. *IPEC Action Against Child Labor: Highlights 2004*, p. 51.

13. Ibid., p. 52.

14. "An Economic Consideration of Child Labor," *By the Sweat & Toil of Children*, volume VI, U.S. Department of Labor, 2000, p. 81, <http://www.dol.gov/ILAB/media/reports/iclp/sweat6/sweat6.pdf> (March 3, 2007).

15. Ibid.

16. Sudhanshu Joshi, Bupinder Zutshi, and Alok Vajpeyi, "Review of Child Labor, Education, and Poverty Agenda, India Country Report Global March Against Child Labor," 2006, p. vi, <http://www.globalmarch.org/resourcecentre/countryreports.php3> (January 18, 2006).

17. "Fact Sheet—Global: Facts on Child Labour," International Labour Organization, <http://www.ilo.org/dyn/declaris/DECLARATIONWEB.INDEXPAGE> (February 25, 2007).

18. "Conversations with Former Working Children: Julekha Akhter," *Advancing the Global Campaign Against Child Labor: Progress Made and Future Actions*, U.S. Department of Labor, ILAB, May 17, 2000, <http://www.dol.gov/ilab/media/reports/iclp/globcamp/globcampconf.htm> (March 4, 2007).

19. *IPEC Action Against Child Labor: Highlights 2004*, p. 20.

20. Ibid., p. 34.

21. Christopher Wakiraza, "Kids in Need: An NGO Solution," *eJournal USA, Economic Perspectives*, May 2005, <http://usinfo.state.gov/journals/journals.htm> (February 6, 2006), pp. 29–30.

22. Patrick del Vecchio, "Child Labor in Brazil: The Government Commitment," *eJournal USA, Economic Perspectives*, May 2005, pp. 27–28, <http://usinfo.state.gov/journals/ites/0505/ijee/delveccio.htm> (March 4, 2007).

23. Ibid.

24. Joshi, Zutshi, and Vajpevi, p. 12.

25. Ibid., p. vi.

26. Ibid., p. 14.

27. Lakshmidhar Mishra, *Child Labor in India* (New York: Oxford University Press, 2000), pp. 106–107.

28. "Stolen Childhoods," transcript, *Nightline: ABC News*, June 15, 2005, p. 3.

29. Dr. Sahib Singh, "Child Labor-Problems and Possible Solutions," Press Information Bureau, Government of India, February 26, 2003, <http://pib.nic.in/feature/feyr2003/ffeb2003/f260220031.html> (October 9, 2005).

30. *The State of the World's Children, 2006 Report*, p. vii.

31. Ibid.

32. "The End of Child Labour: Within Reach," International Labour Organization, pp. 77–79, <http://www.ilo.org/dyn/declaris/DECLARATIONWEB.INDEXPAGE/> (February 25, 2007).

Chapter 8 A Look Ahead

1. Jonathan Silvers, "Child Labor in Pakistan," *The Atlantic Monthly*, February 1996, p. 90.

2. "Reebok and the U.S. Fund for UNICEF Partner to Help Put Child Laborers in School: The 'Fund for Iqbal' is Created in Memory of Slain Child Activist," PR Newswire, May 6, 2004.

3. Ibid.

4. "Pakistan Human Rights Practices, 1995," U.S. Department of State, March 1996, <http://dosfan.lib.uic.edu/ERC/democracy/1995_hrp_report/95hrp_report_sasia/Pakistan.html> (March 5, 2007).

5. "Reebok and the U.S. Fund for UNICEF Partner to Help Put

Child Laborers in School: The 'Fund for Iqbal' is Created in Memory of Slain Child Activist."

6. "A Bullet Can't Kill a Dream," The Kids Campaign to Build, Broad Meadows Middle School, n.d., <http://www.digitalrag.com/iqbal/index.html> (March 4, 2007).

7. Craig Kielburger, *Free the Children* (New York: HarperCollins, 1998), p. 314.

8. "If We Ruled the World," *Guardian Unlimited*, May 12, 2002, <http://www.childrens-express.org/dybnamic/public/if_we_ruled_120502.htm> (March 30, 2006).

9. Ibid.

10. "A World Fit for Children," United Nations General Assembly, October 11, 2002, <http://www.unicef.org/specialsession/docs_new/documents/A-RES-S27-2E.pdf> (March 27, 2007).

11. Manfred Liebel, Bernd Overwien, and Albert Recknagel, eds., *Working Children's Protagonism: Social Movements and Empowerment in Latin America, Africa and India* (Frankfurt: IKO, 2001), pp. 184–185.

12. Ibid.

13. "The Alternate Report," National Movement of Working Children, India, July 2003, <www.workingchild.org/prota12.htm> (February 18, 2007).

14. Liebel, Overwien, Recknagel, pp. 200–204.

15. Ibid., p. 198.

16. Kielburger, p. 312.

17. "Stolen Childhoods," transcript, *Nightline: ABC News*, June 15, 2005, p. 6.

18. "The End of Child Labour: Within Reach," International Labour Organization, p. 21, <http://www.ilo.org/dyn/declaris/DECLARATIONWEB.INDEXPAGE/> (February 25, 2007).

Glossary

bonded labor—A type of slavery. Employers offer a loan to a family or individual who must then work to pay it back.

boycott—A form of protest in which consumers agree not to buy or use a product, bringing pressure on the manufacturer or retailer who offers it.

convention—An understanding or agreement between countries.

Convention on the Rights of the Child (CRC)—An international treaty that states the civil, political, and human rights of children; adopted by the United Nations General Assembly on November 20, 1989.

International Labour Organization (ILO)—An agency of the United Nations that regulates international labor laws. The organization is made up of 179 member states. The goal of the organization is to promote peace and social justice by protecting workers' rights.

International Program for the Elimination of Child Labor (IPEC)—A group within the International Labour Organization devoted to ending child labor.

microfinance—Financial programs that offer credit and loans to poor families.

Millennium Development Goals—Eight goals established at the Millennium Summit in September 2000: to end extreme poverty and hunger; provide universal primary education; promote equality for women and girls; reduce the number of children who die young; improve health standards for mothers; fight diseases such as HIV/AIDS; take care of the environment; and encourage nations to cooperate with one another.

nongovernmental organizations (NGOs)—Humanitarian organizations that do not operate as part of a government agency.

ratify—To agree to the terms of a treaty and promise to obey it.

slavery—Modern-day slavery means to force someone to do a job in exchange for very little pay or no payment at all. Often slavery involves threats or abuse. Types of slavery include bonded labor and trafficking.

stipend—A small payment to help parents send their children to school. When a child stops working, the family loses money. The stipend makes up for the lost income.

trafficking—Moving people from one place to another and forcing them to work.

United Nations Children's Fund (UNICEF)—An agency created by the United Nations in 1946 to provide humanitarian aid to children throughout the world.

United Nations (UN)—A cooperative organization made up of 191 member states, formed after World War II to promote peace and seek solutions to social problems, including emergencies and human rights issues.

World Bank Group—A group of five international institutions that provides loans, grants, and other services to poor and developing countries. The World Bank is made up of two of the five—the International Bank for Reconstruction and Development (IBRD) and the International Development Association (IDA), which are owned by 185 member countries.

Further Reading

Bartoletti, Susan Campbell. *Growing Up in Coal Country.* Boston: Houghton Mifflin, 1999.

Chambers, Catherine. *Living as a Child Laborer: Mehboob's Story.* Milwaukee, Wisc.: World Almanac Library, 2006.

Hopkinson, Deborah. *Shutting Out the Sky: Life in the Tenements of New York, 1880–1924.* New York: Orchard Books, 2003.

Kielburger, Craig, and Kevin Major. *Free the Children: A Young Man Fights Against Child Labor and Proves That Children Can Change the World,* Toronto, M&S, 1999.

Kuklin, Susan. *Iqbal Masih and the Crusaders Against Child Slavery.* New York: Henry Holt and Company, 1998.

Manheimer, Ann. *Child Labor and Sweatshops.* San Diego: Greenhaven Press, 2005.

Newman, Shirlee P. *Child Slavery in Modern Times.* New York: Franklin Watts, 2000.

Roberts-Davis, Tanya. *We Need to Go To School: Voices of the Rugmark Children.* Toronto: Douglas & MacIntyre, 2001.

Shoveller, Herb. *Ryan and Jimmy: And the Well in Africa That Brought Them Together.* Toronto: Kids Can Press, 2006.

Internet Addresses

Free The Children
   <http://www.freethechildren.com>

International Labour Organization
   <http://www.ilo.org>

UNICEF—Voices of Youth
   <http://www.unicef.org/voy>

Index